SPEAKING TRUTH IN LOVE

Speaking Truth in Love: Counsel in Community

David Powlison

New Growth Press

www.newgrowthpress.com

© 2005 by David Powlison

Requests for information should be addressed to:
New Growth Press, P.O. Box 9805, Greensboro, NC 27429-0805.

Scripture quotations are from the NEW AMERICAN STANDARD BIBLE ®. © Copyright The Lockman Foundation 1960, 1962, 1963, 1968, 1971, 1972, 1973, 1975, 1977, 1995. Used by permission.

Italics in Scripture quotations indicate emphasis added.

ISBN-10: 0-9770807-14
ISBN-13: 978-0-9770807-1-7

Printed in Canada

To Dodie Powlison,
my mother and a most companionable friend,
with a lifetime of gratitude for your eminent good sense

CONTENTS

Preface: Good Intentions   1

Part I: Speaking Truth in Love   5
Chapter 1 Suffering and Psalm 119   11
Chapter 2 The Facts of Life   33
Chapter 3 Hearing the Music of the Gospel   41
Chapter 4 How Healthy Is Your Preparation?   49
Chapter 5 What Questions Do You Ask?   55
Chapter 6 Think Globally, Act Locally   61
Chapter 7 Illustrative Counseling   73
Chapter 8 Talk Incessantly? Listen Intently!   83
Chapter 9 How Do You Help a "Psychologized" Counselee? 89

Part II: We Grow Up Together   99
Chapter 10 What Is "Ministry of the Word"?   103
Chapter 11 Counseling Is the Church   109
Chapter 12 What Will You Ask For?   117
Chapter 13 Pastoral Counseling   127
Chapter 14 Counseling Under the
    Influence of the X Chromosome   133
Chapter 15 Do You Ever Refer?   141
Chapter 16 Why I Chose Seminary for
    Counseling Training   153
Chapter 17 Affirmations and Denials   167
    Closing Essay: Companions on the Long March   187

Notes   195
Scripture Index   201

PREFACE

GOOD INTENTIONS

We pray for you always, that our God will . . . fulfill every
desire for goodness and the work of faith with power.
(2 Thess. 1:11)

It's hard enough to think right, but it's harder to live right.
This is a book on how we are to live together. What ought to be
the quality and dynamic of our relationships with each other?
What is right and true, good and loving, lovely and desirable?
We want that.

This book is also about how we *can* live. Of course our
achievements will be imperfect, halting, erratic. But we can do
this to some measure by the grace of God. We can go forward
in this direction and grow in these ways. Any progress at all is
solid joy, lasting treasure, radiant wisdom. We want that.

This book is also about how we *will* live. When all that we
can now barely imagine becomes reality, we will fully savor
what we have already tasted. No eye has seen, no ear has heard,
and no heart has imagined what God has prepared for those
who love him – yet he lets us glimpse, overhear, and catch a
sense of things. We want that.

This book is about how we treat each other, how we work
together, how we help each other. It's about constructive relationships: how we counsel and encourage one another. It's
about what church really is: how we all grow up together. Paul's
request early in 2 Thessalonians recognizes that even our *desire*

for what's right counts. It's better to want what's right than to want what's wrong, or not to know what's right, or not to care. We may fall short of turning intention into action, but intentions matter. Even our "willing of his good pleasure," wanting what is right, is something God works in us. In effect, we can ask, "Our Father, please make our good intentions actually happen, for your sake."

This is a book of good intentions. A James Ward song puts it this way: "Faith takes a vision, turns a dream into a mission." This book presents vision seeking realization in mission. I will describe a *direction* and trace out a few steps in that direction. Direction matters. In effect, we can ask, "Lord, for your name's sake, please make the work that faith imagines a reality."

COUNSEL AND COUNSELING

Speaking Truth in Love is the second in a series. It builds upon *Seeing with New Eyes*.[1] That previous book was an attempt to think right. I sought to bring Scripture to life and to reinterpret common life struggles through God's gaze. It was about "counsel," the content of truth. This second book is about "counsel*ing*," the process of love. Part I will wrestle out how to speak the truth in love in order to do counseling ministry well. Part II will hammer out ways to shape and reshape communities of faith in order to do church well. In other words, this second book describes living right. We will glimpse essential dynamics of relationship and sketch the shape of communities that pursue such relationships.

It's hard to *do counseling ministry well*. How do we converse with others to make the right kind of difference? How do we understand the problems of life so that we can offer real help? We all know that wise, mutual, life-changing counseling means that "speaking the truth in love, we . . . grow up . . . [speak] only such a word as is good for edification according to the need of the moment, so that it will give grace to those who hear . . . encourage one another day after day" (as Ephesians 4 and Hebrews 3 put it). But *how* do we do something so easy to say and so hard to do? A counseling model designs relationships and methods to facilitate the change process; it is counsel*ing* as well as counsel.

It's hard to *do church well*. Church so easily becomes . . . well, becomes "church" (you fill in whatever ruts are most familiar). But if Jesus is full of grace and truth, it must be possible to form communities more full of grace and truth. The flourishing of wise, mutual, life-changing counseling is one proof that everything else about church is accomplishing what it's supposed to. Every counseling model entails a "delivery system," a social structure. Ideas and practices inhabit *institutions*. The most magnificent institutional structure imaginable is a community living out how Ephesians 4 weds pastoral leadership with every-member mutuality.

This book is not an exposition of Ephesians 4 – or, more exactly, of the words we now identify as Ephesians 3:14 to 5:2. But that is the thought unit that most shapes these pages. Grab a handful of verses in either direction from Ephesians 4 – we might call it "Ephesians 4+" – and you capture to perfection a half dozen questions that fill libraries with books. These questions ponder the dance between God's immediate power and our significant choices, between our dependent faith and our active love, between individual experience and the dynamics of the social group, between leadership and mutuality within the social group, between the relationally destructive dynamics of sin and the constructive dynamics of gracious love, between remnant sin and emergent love. These are six perennially perplexing questions. Paul does not so much "answer" them as illustrate how the answers work out in reality. These words from Christ via his messenger will occasionally be visible, but they will always provide the living, invisible structure that informs this book. We might say that Ephesians 4+ forms the neuro-electrical grid, cardiovascular network, and musculo-skeletal system for everything in the pages that follow. In that spectacular revelation, we witness the essential elements of a church functioning as a community characterized by the dynamics of fruitful mutual counseling.

Or we might put it the other way. *Speaking Truth in Love* seeks to recapture how the dynamics of fruitful mutual counseling characterize a church that functions as a community.

PART I   SPEAKING TRUTH IN LOVE

I suppose that all of us who try to help people find ourselves marveling at how mere words, the simplest actions, and the most subtle interpersonal attitudes can have such profound effects on others. Human beings affect each other – for good or ill. If we want to help, not harm, we must consider what affects others for good.

All of us have experienced how an insightful, humane voice can work for good in our lives. (And certainly all of us have experienced how false or callous voices have harmful effects.) It is a fine thing when another human being takes you seriously. Someone wants to know how you are really doing, listens to what you say, and cares enough to respond constructively, saying what is both true and helpful. By word and deed in relationship, one person truly helps another.

LOVE IN ACTION

Wise counseling embodies the human and humane impact of relevant truth. It gives a new perspective and opens up new choices. It both sustains and redirects. For decades, counselors of all stripes have debated the question: Is counseling essentially a matter of *technique* or is it essentially an *art*? Of course, there are elements both of craftsmanship and artistry, but neither is the core. Wise counseling is essentially a way of loving another person well. It is a way of speaking what is true and constructive into *this* person's life right now. Good counseling is essentially wise love in action. It is the image of God made flesh among us, full of grace and truth. Questions of love and truth are foundational and primary for understanding how to counsel. Questions of methodology and artistry are significant but secondary.

Wise love is often both skillful and creative, but it cannot be reduced to a skill set or to creative imagination. I have seen wrecked lives changed simply because a friend cared and was willing to speak honestly like this: "I love and respect you as a person, and I want what is good for you. But you are destroying yourself with what you believe and how you are living." Those were precisely the words that changed *my* life. The cruise missile of wise love blew apart the bunker of self-will in which I lived. My friend's words were not a product of technique. They were artless. But they had four things going for them. They were true, loving, personal, and appropriate.

The living God himself brought my friend's words home with power. He was right. Out of the collapse of core willfulness, I could hear for the first time the voice of another, even greater friend: "I will give you a new heart and put a new spirit within you; and I will remove the heart of stone from your flesh and give you a heart of flesh" (Ezek. 36:26). This Wonderful Counselor's approach is best described as true, loving, personal, appropriate – rather than by categories describing technique, skill set, methodology, or imaginative intuition. Speaking the truth in love comes first. And those words of the Life-giver, the merciful Shepherd, my Father, were precisely the words that changed my life forever.

COUNSELING: PURPOSE, PERSON AND PROCESS

Part I of this book focuses on the counseling conversation between two (or more) people. We will explore several elements that make such conversations fruitful. Think of these chapters as a series of core samples, not a complete excavation of the construction site. I'm not trying to present a model but to give a feel for what it looks like, thinks like, and talks like to counsel biblically. Each chapter is a "for instance," not one segment of a textbook.[1]

But there is a logic to the progression of these nine chapters. The first three concentrate on what you bring to the table as you enter into counseling relationships. Do you know where you are going? What you are aiming for and why? Who you are and your role? The later chapters portray the actual questioning, and listening, and responding. What are you listening for? What do you say? What makes a substantial difference in another person's life?

I think of Chapter 1 as the "Surprise!" in this book. "Suffering and Psalm 119" turns upside down how we think about "counseling." It is my favorite chapter. By instinct, habit, and enculturation, all of us tend to think of counseling as a human-with-human interaction. But in fact a human-with-Savior interaction must come first. When I as a counselor don't get that straight, I inevitably offer others some sort of saviorette. If my counseling does not help others rely upon Another (upon whom I also rely), I will inevitably teach them to rely on themselves – or on me, or other friends, or medications, or techniques, or pablum "truths" (that are in fact empty or even fictional). This cornerstone chapter explores Psalm 119: "If your law had not been my delight, then I would have perished in my affliction" (v. 92).

Chapter 2, "The Facts of Life," explores our resistance to knowing ourselves. Wise counseling helps people face themselves honestly. It helps them look in the only true mirror: What does God see in me? It helps people look suffering in the eye: What is the scene in which God has placed me, and how am I going to respond? We humans fiercely resist seeing ourselves as God sees us. The breaking of our resistance to that light opens the door to God's goodness, intimacy, and grace.

Chapter 3, "Hearing the Music of the Gospel," brings in a third essential ingredient. People who relate their lives to God and who look evils in the eye need something: grace. You can't do life right without the mercies of God in Christ. Wise counseling knows that and brings it. We don't just need a perspective or a strategy. We need a Savior, right here, right now.

The first three chapters tackle the largest matters concerning what you bring to the table in any counseling conversation. Chapter 4 explores the tiniest matters. "How Healthy is Your Preparation?" looks at the simple things you do to prepare to talk to another human being. Your responses to those larger issues are revealed in these little corners of life.

From your foundation, the ten thousand particulars of wise counseling method are built. Chapter 5 moves into the actual human-with-human interaction. "What Questions Do You Ask?" uncovers the deeper questions that must thread through the swarms of particular questions and comments by which you get to know another person. The most commonplace questions – "What happened?" "How do you feel about that?" "What is your problem?" "What do you think would make a difference?" – are altered when we align our agenda with the way that Jesus Christ probes people.

Chapter 6, "Think Globally, Act Locally," presents a case study in how to use Scripture within a counseling conversation. By necessity, to be human means that we do not live by bread alone, but by every word that proceeds from the mouth of God. Wise counseling must be biblical counseling. Counseling that offers no word from God will parch, starve, mislead, and ultimately kill the very people it tries hard to help. But how does counseling present and work with Scripture?

"Illustrative Counseling" (Chapter 7) provides one small illustration of how "speaking the truth in love" gets up close and personal. Biblical counseling is not the mere citation and recitation of Bible verses (any more than biblical preaching is). Truth always adapts, comes down to earth, wears the clothes of this person's life experience. Listen well to people, and you will find stories and metaphors that will help you to speak well into their lives.

Chapter 8 takes up the problem of how to talk with people who talk-talk-talk-talk-talk. Have you ever tried to converse with someone who talks at you? Such monologues make for some of the most maddening counseling imaginable. "Talk Incessantly? Listen Intently!" works on how to turn monologues into dialogue.

Chapter 9 takes on a problem common in contemporary western cultures. You will counsel people who have already been listening hard to other counselors. Those counselors have persuasively misinterpreted life and earnestly offered saviorettes. "How Do You Help a 'Psychologized' Counselee?" considers a woman who needs to radically reframe the way she understands herself, her sufferings, her motives, and her God.

I   SUFFERING AND PSALM 119

I would have perished in my affliction if your words had not been my delight.

When you hear the words "Psalm 119," what are your first associations?

I suspect that your heart does *not* immediately come up with the following: "Psalm 119 is where I go to learn how to open my heart about what matters, to the person I most trust. I affirm what I most deeply love. I express pure delight. I lay my sufferings and uncertainties on the table. I cry out in need and shout for joy. I hear how to be forthright without self-righteousness. I hear how to be weak without self-pity. I learn how true honesty talks with God: fresh, personal, and direct; never formulaic, abstract, or vague. I hear firsthand how Truth and honesty meet and talk it over. This Truth is never denatured, rigid, or inhuman. This honesty never whines, boasts, rages, or gets defensive. I leave the conversation nourished by the sweetest hope imaginable. I hear how to give full expression to what it means to be human, in honest relationship with the Person who made humanness in his image."

Such a response reflects that Truth has grappled with everything you think, feel, do, experience, and need, changing the way you process life. And *you* have grappled with Truth. Imagine, now you can say what you're really thinking and feeling, because insane self-centeredness has been washed away! Such honesty is what Psalm 119 intends to work in you. It is about life's painful realities, the gifts of God, and how those two meet to find life's highest delight.

OTHER REACTIONS

But most people's immediate reaction to Psalm 119 is this: *It's long.* If you're reading through the Bible, you take a deep breath before you trudge through it. It's the same length as the books of Ruth, James, and Philippians. Reading Psalm 119 is too often like watching scenery along an interstate highway. You glimpse lots of things, but you mostly remember the long drive.

Here's a second reaction: *It's repetitive and general.* The verses seem to say the same thing over and over, with few details. In contrast, Ruth tells a moving story. James sparkles with practical application and metaphor. Philippians links wonders about Christ with details of Paul's experience, and then with direct implications for how you and I live. But Psalm 119 seems to drone on in generalities.

Here's another common reaction: *The parts seem uncon-nected.* There is no story line or logical progression. Ruth's sur-prise loyalty to the Lord connects her to a mother-in-law, to a village, to a new husband, to her great-grandson, to the Savior of the world. But Psalm 119 seems like a random collection of disconnected bits.

Or perhaps this Bible fact is one of your associations: *Psalm 119 is not random; it's a tightly structured acrostic.* Twenty-two sections, eight lines each, every line beginning with the same letter, proceeding through the letters of the Hebrew alphabet: *aleph, beth, gimel . . . tav.* The A-to-Z no doubt helped the mem-ory of Hebrew speakers. But it has little relevance for us who read in English, where the alphabetic arrangement gets lost in translation. To us, it is little more than a curiosity.

This association is probably on everyone's list: *It's about God's Word.* Scripture discusses Scripture in almost every verse. It is a classic text on the importance of Bible fidelity, knowl-edge, reading, study, and memorization.

One common negative reaction is that *many people feel bur-dened by it.* The seemingly relentless read-your-Bible-memorize-

Scripture emphasis can come across as moralistic. Your relationship with the Lord seems to hinge on the dutiful performance of "quiet time," but somehow you never get it right. Unlike the warm, intimate promises of favorite psalms like 23, 103, 121, and 139, this psalm can seem biblicistic – that is, it has a reputation for substituting devotion to the Bible for devotion to God. This is a bad rap, but it reflects how Psalm 119 is often misread, mistaught, and misused.

More positively, *perhaps you think of a beloved verse or two.* Maybe verse 11 is on your list of memorable Scripture: "I have hidden your word in my heart that I might not sin against you." Maybe verse 18 shapes your prayers: "Open my eyes, Lord, that I might behold wondrous things out of your law." Maybe verse 67 summarizes the good that came out of suffering: "Before I was afflicted I went astray, but now I keep your word." Or verse 105 might be a song in your heart: "Thy word is a lamp unto my feet and a light unto my path."

Each of these associations is plausible. But most don't lead to the candid conversation described earlier. Psalm 119 itself does lead in that direction. Let's see how it gets there so that we can follow along.

THE HEART OF THE PSALM

Let's begin with a question: "What words are most frequently repeated in Psalm 119?" The answer that usually comes to mind? "It's about the Word of God. Almost every verse contains a word describing what's written in the Bible: *word, law, commandment, precept, testimony, statute, judgment.*"

But when you look more closely, the words describing Scripture run a distant second. Far and away the most common words are first and second person singular pronouns: *I, me, my, mine, and you, your, yours.*[1] Psalm 119 is the most extensive I-to-you conversation in the Bible. Only the first three verses talk *about* people-in-general, *about* God, and *about* the Word, stating propositions and principles in the third person: "Blessed are *those* who observe *his* testimonies, who seek *him* with all *their* heart." The fourth verse begins to personalize things: we stand accountable to *you*. After that, for the next 172 verses, *I, your servant, talk to you, LORD, who speaks and acts, whom I need and love.*[2]

In other words, Psalm 119 is personal prayer. It's talking to, not teaching about. We hear what a man says out loud in God's presence: his joyous pleasure, vocal need, open adoration, blunt requests, candid assertions, deep struggles, fiercely good intentions. The various words for the Word appear once in each verse, but I-you words appear about four times per verse. That's a 4:1 ratio and emphasis.

So Psalm 119 is actually not about the topic of getting Scripture into your life. Instead, it is the honest words that erupt when what God says gets into you. It's not an exhortation to Bible study; it's an outcry of faith.

This makes a world of difference in how you relate to Psalm 119. A topic is abstract, informing the intellect to influence the will. It can be interesting, informative, and even persuasive. But Psalm 119 springs from a man already persuaded. He simply talks, fusing his intellect, will, emotions, circumstances, desires, fears, needs, memory, and anticipation. He's keenly aware of what he's really like and what's happening to him. He's keenly aware of the Lord and the relevance of what God sees, says, and does. This makes his heart tumble out in passionate requests and affirmations. He persuades us not by argument, but by infectious faith.

Psalm 119 is torrential, not topical. It's relentless, not repetitive. It's personal, not propositional. Yes, the form of Psalm 119 is regular. But why this tight discipline of *aleph* to *tav*, the arithmetic regularities that pattern the vocabulary, the unvarying reference back to Scripture? These provide the crucible that contains, purifies, channels, and pours forth molten, living gold. Psalm 119 is the thoughtful outcry that rises when real life meets real God.

It's not just naked candor. Raw honesty is always perverted by the insanity of sin. Should you "get in touch with your feelings and say what you really think"? You do need to face what is going on in yourself and your world. And the opposites of honesty are other madnesses: indifference, busyness, stoicism, niceness, ignorance, self-deception, or denial. But how will you interpret what you feel? Where will you go with it? Honesty in the raw is always godless, willful, opinionated, self-centered. And personal honesty never actually faces reality if it does not simultaneously face God: "A fool finds no pleasure in understanding, but delights in airing his own opinions" (Prov. 18:2). Psalm 119 demonstrates the salvation of honesty. When you truly face yourself, your circumstances, and God, even painful honesty takes on the sanity of Jesus.

Reading, studying, and memorizing the Bible are legitimate implications of Psalm 119 when they aim for this desired result. But this passage really aims to rescript the inner logic and intentionality of your heart. That profound result is not an automatic consequence of rubbing shoulders with the Bible. We have a tendency to mishear what God says, to misapply it, and to mistake means for ends. This psalm demonstrates the radical end.

So this is what we hear in Psalm 119. *A person who has listened* opens his heart to the Person who has spoken. A person who has listened *opens his heart* to the Person who has spoken. A person who has listened opens his heart *to the Person who has spoken.* And this is what he says:

- He boldly asserts who the Lord is.
- He lays his life on the table, both his inner struggle and what comes at him from the outside.
- He pleads for God's help in life's fundamental troubles.
- He asserts his core convictions, affirming his identity, his hope, and his delight.

These four components of what-I-say-to-You are the intertwining strands that form this psalm's inner logic.

STRAND 1: "YOU ARE . . . , YOU SAY . . . , YOU DO . . . "

This speaker describes God to his face: what you're like, what you say and do, who you are. Many psalms develop one memorable theme. Psalm 119 scatters truths with abandon.

Imagine Psalm 119 as a crowded wedding reception, held in a vast banquet hall from which numerous doors lead to other rooms. People you mostly don't know are sitting at tables for eight. The seating arrangement is odd. The bride's grandmother is sitting next to the groom's college roommate, simply because their last names both start with S! How will you ever get to know all those individual faces, names, stories? But stop at each table. Ask questions, listen, and get acquainted.

You discover that a rich confession of faith is strewn throughout Psalm 119. Its form is startling. It's not phrased as the faith you profess: "I believe in God the Father. I believe in Jesus Christ. I believe in the Holy Spirit." It's faith heard in the act of confessing: "You are my Father. You are my Savior. You are my Life-giver."

The Lord has arranged the conditions of my existence.

- You established the earth, and it stands.
- All things are your servants.
- The earth is full of your lovingkindness.
- Your faithfulness continues through all generations.
- Your hands made me and fashioned me.
- I am your servant.
- I am yours.
- All my ways are before you.
- You are near.

The Lord speaks wonders.
- Your law is truth.
- Your testimonies are wonderful.
- Your word is pure.
- Your word stands firm in the heavens forever.
- The unfolding of your words gives light.
- Your word is a lamp to my feet and a light to my path.

The Lord destroys evil.
- You rebuke the arrogant.
- You reject those who wander from your statutes.
- You will execute judgment on those who persecute me.
- You have removed all the wicked of the earth like dross.

Yet the Lord is merciful to me.
- You are good and do good.
- In faithfulness you afflicted me.
- Your mercies are great.
- You comfort me.
- You are my hiding place and my shield.
- You answered me.
- You have dealt well with your servant.
- You have revived me.
- You will enlarge my heart.
- You yourself have taught me.

How did the psalmist learn to be so outspoken to God? He listened to what God said in the rest of the Bible, and lived it. The Lord says who he is, and is who he says. The Lord says what he does, and does what he says. Faith listens, experiences what is true, and talks back in simple sentences.

We tend to be busy, noisy, distractible people in a busy, noisy, distracting world. This psalm teaches us to say, "I need time to listen and think if I'm ever to converse with God." In a culture of instant information, this psalm rewards the slow. If you speed-read, all you get is, "Psalm 119 is about the Bible." But if you take it slow and live it out, you find yourself saying things like this: "You are good and do good." Or this: "I am yours." Learning to say that out loud and mean it will change your life forever.

Here's another implication. Our self-help culture is preoccupied with "self-talk." Does what you say to yourself cheer you up or tear you down? Do you say, "I'm a valid person and I can stand up for myself," or "I'm so stupid and I always fail"? Entire systems of counseling revolve around reconstructing self-talk so you'll be happier and more productive. But Psalm 119 gets you out of the monologue business entirely. It gets you talking with the Person whose opinion finally matters. The problem with self-talk is that we aren't talking to anyone but ourselves. A conversation ought to be taking place, but we repress our awareness of the Person who threatens our self-fascination.

The Bible says radical things about the stream of consciousness that talks inside us: "Every intention of the thoughts of his heart was only evil all the days" (Gen. 6:5); "All his thoughts are, 'There is no God'" (Ps. 10:4).[3] This does not only refer to vile lifestyles. It includes the everyday ways our minds operate without reference to God. Functional atheism is our most natural state of mind.

Our self-talk is usually like the people who talk to themselves on the subway. Their world is real to them, but it's disconnected from everyone else. We talk in our sleep. The dreams might be pleasant. They might be nightmares. But either way, it's a dream. The vocal faith of Psalm 119 is what happens when you wake up. The stream of false consciousness becomes a stream of conscious awareness, love, trust, and need. Sanity makes clear affirmations to the Person whose attitude and actions are decisive.

I've likened Psalm 119 to a wedding reception full of guests. But notice also the doors leading to other rooms. Psalm 119 breaks out toward the rest of Scripture. How did this man learn to say with all his heart, "You are good and do good"? Where did he learn, "I am yours"? Psalm 119 carries you to the rest of God's revelation and to all of life. Eight summary words for his words, each used about twenty-two times, act as pointers.

Word

Two of the eight words simply mean *word*, everything God talks about. His words are all he says and writes. Understand this and you'll never treat Psalm 119 in a moralistic way. What is contained in all these different words? We hear stories, commands, promises, a worldview interpreting all that happens. We witness who God is, what he is like, what he does. He promises mercies. He warns of consequences. He tells us who we are, why we do what we do, what is at stake in our lives, what he made us for. He identifies what's wrong with us. Through story and precept, he teaches us the meaning of sufferings and blessings. He tells us exactly what he expects from us. His words reveal his lovingkindness. And so forth.

So what does it mean then to say, I "keep your word" (v.17)? The obvious example is obedience to specific commandments.

You keep "Do not commit adultery" by not committing adultery. How do you keep other sorts of words, like, "In the beginning God created the heavens and the earth"? You keep them by believing, remembering, and changing how you look at everything. Our psalm keeps Genesis 1 by affirming to God, "*You* established the earth, and it stands. All things are *your* servants." That's faith in action. You keep Genesis 1 by remembering that you, too, are a dependent creature whose purposes are accountable to your Maker. You are not merely your résumé, your feelings, your relationships, your bank account, your plans, or your experiences. Our psalm says, "*Your* hands made me and fashioned me. I am *yours*."

Law

Another of the eight words is *law*. This also means *everything* God says. It's a synonym for *word* – with special emphasis on the Lord's authority and our need to listen. It means teaching we must heed. *Law* is identical to *word* in scope but richer in nuance. It highlights the personal authority of the Savior-King.

We tend to mishear *law* when we read Psalm 119. We depersonalize it into a law code unrelated to God's gracious rule. We narrow *law* to bare-bones commandments, forgetting that "ten commandments" is a misnomer. Those "ten words"[4] reveal our Lord's creating and saving acts, his lovingkindness, generous gifts, good character, promises, warnings, and calling of a people – the interpersonal context for his ten good commands. We forget that these commandments spell out how love works out towards God and our fellow human beings. We forget that the law of Moses includes teaching like this: "The LORD, the LORD God, compassionate and gracious, slow to anger, and abounding in lovingkindness and truth; who keeps lovingkindness for thousands, who forgives iniquity, transgression and sin; yet he will by no means leave the guilty unpunished" (Ex. 34:6-7). When a person like this gives commandments, he spells out how to become just like him.

Obedience lives out this wise love on a human scale. In the new covenant, Jesus does what we fail to do. He loves as a neighbor and friend. He loves as the Lamb of God, sacrificed in our place. He loves as one of us, the pioneer and perfecter of faith working through love. God writes this law of love on our hearts. The Father and the Son come to live within us, by the Holy Spirit, and we learn to love – this law fulfilled.

Psalm 119 opens with a stunning benediction: "Blessed are those whose way is blameless, who walk in the law of the LORD." The convergence between our highest happiness and our wholehearted goodness sets the stage for everything that follows. So what does it mean to "walk in" the Lord's law? It means, "Love God utterly (free from a willful heart) – because he loves you. Love other people (free from compulsive selfishness) – the same way he loves you." To obey God's will is to love well because you are loved well.

We rarely think through what it means to "walk in" other parts of this comprehensive teaching. This law says, "The Lord bless you and keep you; the Lord make his face shine on you and be gracious to you; the Lord lift up his face on you and give you peace" (Num 6:24-26). You walk in this by asking God to treat you this way. You receive. You trust. You treat others in these same ways, as a living conduit of care, grace, and peace. No wonder our psalm proclaims, "I love your law. Your law is my delight."

Judgments

Judgments (or "ordinances") put the emphasis on how God evaluates things. They teach us to weigh things for what they actually are. For example, in God's judgment, cheating on your spouse is wrong. In God's judgment, trusting in the grace of Christ is the way of forgiveness and life. In God's judgment, compassion for helpless people demonstrates the goodness of his character. In God's judgment, dealing gently with the ignorant and wayward demonstrates his mercy. In God's judgment, he alone is the only wise God.

Interestingly, two of the handful of verses in Psalm 119 that lack a direct reference to God's Word contain the word "judgment," but not as a reference to what is written. They describe the actions that flow from good judgment, and so bring about justice (vv. 84, 121). In several other places, Psalm 119's reference to "judgments" could mean either what God said about things or what he does in acting on how he judges things to be. The end point and goal of Psalm 119 is not the Bible; the end point of the Bible is life.

Testimony, Precepts, Statutes, Commandments

And so it continues, each synonym adding its richness to the unified picture. God's *testimony* speaks of everything to which he bears witness. He witnesses to himself, to right and wrong, to human failings, to human good, to his saving actions, to his creation of the world, to his will. Those "ten words" we mentioned are frequently called "the testimony," bearing witness to what is true, right, and delightful. *Precepts* give detailed practical instructions that help us understand exactly what it looks like for us to believe, do, and delight.

Statutes capture the fact that all these things are written down. They are standing truth, standing orders, a permanent constitution. God affixes his words on stone tablets, scrolls, books, computers – that he might write his words on hearts. *Commandments* tell you exactly how to live, what to do, how to love and trust. Because God's words come with authority, they all have the character of a command even when God promises mercy, reveals his character, or tells a story of what he did: you *must* believe it and live out the implications. Every alternative is some species of self-deception and destruction.

How do we react to all these things? The verbs in Psalm 119 are consistent: "I keep, I seek, I love, I choose, I remember, I do, I believe, I rejoice in, I meditate on, I cling to, I delight in, I do not forget. . . . I respond in all these ways to your word, law, judgments, testimonies, precepts, statutes, and command-ments." Every aspect of the word of life elicits the same family of reactions. Plain speaking to God about God is one result.

Strand 2: "I Am Facing a Struggle With . . ."

Were you surprised by the title of this chapter, "*Suffering* and Psalm 119"? Other psalms are more obviously cries for mercy and protection. But Psalm 119 is thought to be about moral and intellectual self-discipline, not the anguish of life. The reputation is wrong. Psalm 119 is spoken out of ongoing struggle. This discipline of heart and mind arises in the midst of battle.

Struggle appears in each of the twenty-two sections. What does this man find so difficult, so troubling, so painful, so threatening and dangerous?

Let me state it in first person words. First, I face something terrible inside myself. My own sinfulness means that God could destroy me. Second, I face something terrible coming at me. The sins of others and life's troubles threaten my life.

Either way, whether sin or hurt, I suffer threats of pain, shame, and death. So I talk candidly to God about my double affliction. My suffering goes deep. Psalm 119 teaches you to say things like: "My soul cleaves to the dust. My soul weeps because of grief. My eyes fail. When will you comfort me?"

Scripture uses the word "evil" the same way we use it in English, to describe both sins and troubles. The problem of evil is in me and comes at me. It perverts me and it hurts me. Ecclesiastes 9:3 nails both: "This is the evil [suffering] in all that is done under the sun, that there is one fate for all men. Furthermore, the hearts of the sons of men are full of evil [sin], and insanity is in their hearts while they live [sin], and then they die [suffering]." Psalm 119 struggles with both problems.

First, the psalmist finds evil within himself. The illumination of the Word produces a devastating self-awareness. The torrent of I-to-you speech begins in verse 5. And it is no accident that the opening sentence asks for help. He must cry out, "How can I avoid being ashamed when I look at what you command?" He feels threatened because of his sin's tendencies. He shocks us when the last line of the first section expresses such anxious need, "Do not utterly forsake me!" He again shocks us when the last line of the entire psalm bursts out with this admission, "I have gone astray like a lost sheep."

It is notoriously difficult to discern patterns in the overall flow of Psalm 119. But clearly the placement of verses 8 (the end of the first section) and 176 (the end of the last section) intends to highlight something. This honest man suffers in his sinfulness and longs for deliverance. He must voice this struggle because he takes so personally what he stated categorically in the opening lines:

> How blessed are those whose way is blameless, who walk in the law of the LORD. How blessed are those who observe his testimonies, who seek him with all their heart. They also do no unrighteousness. They walk in his ways. You have ordained your precepts, that we should keep them diligently.

Because this is how life works, his sins grieve and frighten him. Will God utterly forsake me? Will I wander away? Will God rebuke me and curse me? Will I be put to shame? Will I sin? Will I forget? Will I be thrown away? Will I end up consumed by dread, not filled with joy? Will I be accursed by death, not blessed by life? These questions haunt Psalm 119.

Second, he finds evil coming at him. The discipline of the Word of God produces heightened sensitivity. God's sovereign rule and promised grace aggravate a sense of pain, without self-pity: "I am small and despised. Trouble and anguish come upon me. I face oppression and scorn from self-willed people, for no reason but their malice. They are out to get me. They sabotage and persecute me with lies. I've been almost destroyed. I would have perished in my affliction. I don't fit in; I am a stranger here on earth. I lie awake at night. How long can I take it?"

This man voices his struggle because he takes so personally the Lord's lovingkindness. "If you promise blessedness, if you deal bountifully and give life, if you have made me hope in your promises, if your face shines on your servant, if you save me, if you teach me, if you revive me . . . then you must come through for me. What I'm experiencing is so hurtful and threatening. I'm experiencing the opposite of all your goodness."

Notice another pattern in the flow of Psalm 119. The first

two sections and the last make no mention of the pains of life. Two things predominate: the inner struggle of our need for wisdom, and a triumphant joy. But every other section mentions sufferings. Pain and threat are always present, but with one striking exception, they never claim center stage. That exception occurs at the center of the psalm. In verses 81-88, the psalmist hits bottom. He communicates a vivid sense of distress, sinking, vulnerability, and fragility. Then, strikingly, as the psalm passes the mid-point (vv. 89-91), he completely changes direction. Faith's neediness yields to faith's trust. Elsewhere in Psalm 119, he never dwells on any one theme. But here he affirms over and over the Lord's certainty.

> Forever, O LORD, your word is settled in heaven. Your faithfulness continues throughout all generations. You established the earth and it stands. They stand this day according to your ordinances, for all things are your servants.

There's nothing else like that in Psalm 119. It arises from the ashes of distress. His hope speaks within the fragility of his situation and steps into light. He summarizes what has happened with words paraphrased in the title of this chapter: "If your law had not been my delight, then I would have perished in my affliction" (v. 92).

Evils within, evils without – both animate this man of sorrows. Such candid godliness is quite different from the popular picture of Psalm 119. Does it portray an ideal of unruffled self-discipline, detached from sin and suffering? On the contrary! The Word itself disciplines a person to say, "My soul weeps in grief." The clarity of this man's awareness of God and of what ought to be produces a painful clarity that all is not right. The truth of God produces in him an impassioned sense of need.

STRAND 3: "I NEED YOU TO . . . "

So far we've heard two things. A man speaks to God about God and about his struggle with evil. He puts the two together.

The result? Some eighty or ninety requests for specific help. This is astonishing when you think about it.

First, what is the *usual effect of sufferings*, troubles, and threat? We turn in on ourselves. We brood about what's happening and our world shrinks. In so doing, we implicitly turn away from God – and sometimes even turn overtly against him.

Second, what is the *intrinsic effect of sin* and wandering? We turn in on ourselves and away from God. Even the "little" sins, like complaining, expunge the Lord from his universe. Sin curves in on itself (*curvitas in se,* as the ancients put it).

Third, in those with an active conscience, what is the *usual after-effect of sin*, that painful sense of coming up short? Again, we turn in on ourselves. We brood about what we've done. We hide from God, or despair, or mumble apologies, or redouble good intentions. In short, all evils tend to create monologues in the theater of our own minds.

But Psalm 119 creates a dialogue in the theater of the Lord's universe.[5] We hear cries of specific need in the face of sufferings and sins. This man takes God at his word and asks for what God alone can do. His requests align with his struggles against sin and pain. He wants mercy in both senses of the word. He wants mercy for his sin. He wants mercy in his suffering.

He pleads for God to deliver him from his own failings. As a man with a tender conscience, he asks, "Don't forsake me utterly! Seek your servant!" In other words, "Don't give up on me. Come after me and rescue me."

He knows how hard it is to love. "Don't let me wander from your commandments." He gets preoccupied with the wrong things. "Incline my heart to your testimonies."

His Bible gets routine so that he can read but miss the Lord. "Open my eyes that I may behold wonderful things from your law." He gets hooked on emptiness. "Turn my eyes away from looking at vanity."

Sin can seize control. "Don't let iniquity reign over me." He's vulnerable to bad choices. "Make me walk in the path of your commandments."

He knows he needs mercy. "Be gracious to me according to your word."

Ten times he simply asks, "Teach me." Nine times, "Revive me." Six times, "Make me understand." He knows exactly what God says, and exactly what he needs. It's *because* he knows those wonders of judgment, promise, testimony, and command – and *because* he knows his dull heart, and the distraction of his troubles – that he begs God to make him alive. "I can read it, I can quote it. I want to live it. You must make me do it. You must change me and teach me."

Psalm 119 also pleads for deliverance from painful troubles. As always, he wastes no words.

- Save me.
- Help me.
- Rescue me.
- Plead my cause.
- Look on my affliction.
- When will you comfort me?
- When will you judge those who persecute me?
- Don't let the arrogant oppress me.
- It is time for the Lord to act!

The lovingkindness of the Lord invites such pleas. Poverty? Bereavement? Sickness? Painful dying? Unfairness? Oppression? Betrayal? God cares, and the needy cry out.

Why do books on prayer often seem so gooey in comparison; purveying false promises; creating false expectations; delivering untrue views of God, of us, and of circumstances? Why do they sound so "religious," when this man sounds so real? Why does "prayer" become such a production, or a formula of steps to follow and words to recite, or a heightened state of consciousness, or a superstitious ritual, or a way to be fake, or a way to bend God's ear for personal advantage, or all of the above at the same time? "Teach me. Revive me. Make me different. It is time for the Lord to act!"

When the great Augustine wrote a commentary on the Psalms, he put off Psalm 119 until the end. He kept putting it off until his friends made him write it. Beneath the simple surface, he found this psalm too deep for comment: "It always exceeded the powers of my intent thought and the utmost grasp of my faculties." But what he could not grasp, he was able to live. Certainly it is here that Augustine learned to say, "Give what you command, O Lord, and command what you will." The words tell us what to believe, trust, need, and do – and God must make it so.

STRAND 4: "I AM COMMITTED TO . . . "

We've seen three things: "You are. . . . I'm facing. . . . I ask. . . . " Now, fourth, "Here I stand." Psalm 119 makes numerous statements of faith.

This man states his convictions. He knows who he is and whose he is. He is a child of the light. He will never forget the light and aims to serve it.

- I am yours.
- I am your servant.
- I have promised to keep your words.
- I treasure your word in my heart.
- Now I keep your word.
- Your servant meditates on your statutes.
- I shall keep your statutes.
- I cling to your testimonies.
- I observe your testimonies.
- I have done justice and righteousness.
- I have chosen the faithful way.
- I do not turn aside from your law.
- I have restrained my feet from every evil way.
- I hope for your salvation, O Lord.
- I believe in your commandments.
- I do your commandments.
- I have not forgotten your law.
- I do not forget your commandments.
- I shall not forget your word.
- I will never forget your precepts.

A Christian conscience can say the following things in the

same sentence: "Lord, you seek me out and show mercy because you are good [strand 1]; I have gone astray like a lost sheep and I feel battered and vulnerable [strand 2]; seek your servant [strand 3]; I do not forget your commandments [strand 4]." Living faith includes a simultaneous awareness of God's grace, besetting evils, deep need, and indwelling radiance. "You are merciful," "I am the chief of sinners," "That hurts," "Have mercy," and "I am yours" go well together.

Finally, this honest man voices his delight. Within the conversation of Psalm 119, he gets a lot of what he asks for: firmly anchored joy, clear-sighted direction, utter delight. This man experiences grace working within him. He has been changed, is being changed, and will be changed. He experiences consolation and protection amid his troubles. He has a vivid sense for how God's good purposes work out. Twofold grief over evil drove him in anxious need to the Lord. Twofold delight at good animates his joy. Some forty times, he rejoices, delights, loves, gives thanks, marvels, and sings praise! A person of the Word feels and says things like these:

- My heart stands in awe at everything you've said.
- I love what you say – exceedingly, passionately, above all things.
- I love your commandments more than rivers of gold.
- Your words are sweeter than honey in my mouth.
- Your testimonies are the joy of my heart.
- I absolutely delight in all that you say.
- The things you have written down are my songs.
- I get up at midnight simply to give thanks to you.
- I look forward to lying awake so I can ponder your words.
- I behold wonders in your law because I behold you.

All created things, all commandments, all promises, all stories of your ways with humankind, all events . . . all reveal you; my joy, my hope, my delight; you, my highest exultation; you, my deep and indestructible gladness.

WHAT WILL YOU WALK AWAY WITH?

Psalm 119 is like a vast, crowded room, but it richly rewards our efforts to talk with any of the guests present. Let me give one example. How do you handle a sleepless night? You're lying awake; where do you go in your mind? How do you feel? It just so happens that Psalm 119 mentions being awake at night four times.

> I remember your name in the night and keep your law . . . . At midnight I shall rise to give thanks to you because of your righteous ordinances . . . . I rise before dawn and cry for help; I wait for your words. My eyes anticipate the night watches, that I may meditate on your word. (vv. 55, 62, 147-148)

A sleepless night is not the harshest form of suffering. It brings you down by slow erosion, not devastating landslide. Sleeplessness is tiresome and tiring. That much is obvious.

Now to the less obvious. What *do* you think about when you lie awake at night? Does your mind run to tomorrow? Do you pre-solve every problem that might arise? Does your mind run to yesterday, brooding over your own failures? Do you replay the hurtful videotape of what someone else did or said?

Do you just run away, turning to escapist, feel-good fantasies? Do you lie awash in your hobbies, immorality, athletic dreams, or vacation plans?

Or in the long night hours, do you cycle through anxieties: money, kids, terrorists, singleness, church problems, sickness, loneliness, and lots more? Do you sink into a pool of depressed resignation? Or do you attach all your hopes to some promise of sleep? If you pray, is the focus solely on your desire for sleep, based on Psalm 127:2?

Does Psalm 119 have anything to say about these parking places for the heart? It changes every one. Whether the hours are marked by tedium or swept into some dark frenzy, those hours are largely God-less. Psalm 119 describes hours full of God. It doesn't promise sleep (though rest is a good gift); it promises to change sleeplessness.

Let me make it personal. Until the 1990s I rarely experienced sleeplessness. Then I started to travel each year to Korea. My body clock would get turned around. I'd work a long day, and drop off to sleep around 11:00 P.M., only to awaken and lie awake from 1:30 A.M. until 6:00 A.M., when I had to get up again. My instinctive response was to plow and replow the list of the new day's responsibilities, which led to grumbling and apprehension ("What will the day be like if I am exhausted?"). I hated not sleeping.

But on my third trip to Korea, I happened to read Psalm 119 on the plane. Verse 148 arrested me: "My eyes anticipate the night watches, that I may meditate on your word." Could I face the inevitable night watches with anticipation, not apprehension? God proved true to his word. I awakened on cue that first night, but I went to a new place. I turned over in my mind Psalm 23, and Numbers 6:24-26, the Beatitudes, and Psalm 131, and everything I could remember from Ephesians and John 1. Psalm 119 opened doors into the rest of Scripture. Night after night, I remembered, thought, prayed, trusted, loved, and delighted – and sometimes slept.

Of course, I was still fatigued during the days. Faith is not magic. And I felt no particular delight in being wide awake. Sleeplessness *is* a form of suffering. But the nights had changed.

I learned something – and it soon came to my aid in a far deeper way. After heart surgery in 2000, sleepless hours became a nightly occurrence for a long time. I would rather have slept. But in the darkness, I was loved by God, and I loved him in return. Imagine, in sleeplessness, you are my Shepherd. I lack nothing. You make me lie down in green pastures. You lead me beside still waters. You restore my soul. You lead me in paths of righteousness for your name's sake. Even though I walk through the valley of the shadow of death, I fear no evil, for you are with me. . . . Surely goodness and lovingkindness will follow me all the days of my life. This leaves no part of a sleepless night unchanged.

Where do you need Psalm 119 to help you? Is it sleepless nights? Does some form of lovelessness repeatedly puncture your life – worry, fears, sexual lust, bitterness, lying, temper, procrastination? Where do you need real help, not good intentions or quick fixes? "I am yours. Save me. Teach me."

Is it the sharp-edged pain of some suffering? Have you been betrayed? Is there a rift in a relationship? Is your body failing? Is your child straying? "I would have perished in my affliction."

Does your joy simply need to become more vocal? Does your confession of faith simply need to become more head on? "You are my Father. You established the earth. All things are your servants." Psalm 119 teaches us that way of talking.

Go back through Psalm 119 on your own. Listen for affirmations about God. Listen for struggles and cries of honest need. Listen for expressions of conviction and delight. Find one affirmation about God that you need to voice. Identify one struggle with inner evil or outer pain that maps onto your own struggles. Choose one request that captures what you need God to do. Select one joyous assertion that expresses what you long to become in full.

Psalm 119 is the most "individualistic" psalm. We overhear first person singular faith. But what each one of us experiences, needs, and affirms always spills over into what all of us need, experience, and affirm. As faith works through love, private faith embraces the concerns of all of us together. "Open our eyes, Lord, and we will behold wonderful things in all that you have spoken to us!"

2   THE FACTS OF LIFE

It were an easy thing to be a Christian,
    if religion stood only in a few outward works and duties,
But to take the soul to task,
    and to deal roundly with our own hearts,
    and to let conscience have its full work,
    and to bring the soul into spiritual subjection unto God,
This is not so easy a matter,
    because the soul out of self-love is loath to enter into itself,
    lest it should have other thoughts of itself than it would have.
                    - Richard Sibbes[1]

Striking words, aren't they? This statement – some 400 years old – touches the deepest issues of counseling in any time and place. The soul of every human being is loath to enter into itself because of self-love. None of us wants to acknowledge things about ourselves that we would rather deny. We would really rather not know.

Do you ever talk with people about their problems or about your own? Sibbes's words are a slipper that fits every foot. Perhaps your role is designated by some title that defines you as a counselor. Or you might be "just" a coworker, neighbor, friend, parent, spouse, sibling, child, or grandparent. How do you help a person you love to think straight, when he or she thinks crooked? How do *you* learn to see straight and think straight, when something inside you compulsively bends in the wrong direction?

You need a clear-eyed realism about the human tendency

towards self-blinding. Only then will you bring a buoyant sense of the centrality of the grace of Jesus Christ in counseling ministry. And only then will you help people make the most essential change of all, learning to know God in real life. Those three issues – accurate honesty, living mercy, and daily intimacy – are the focus of the pages that follow.

FACING THE TRUTH ABOUT YOURSELF

Sibbes gets first things first. Jesus' almighty kindness comes to sinful people in order to recreate us as children of God's glory. He remakes us poor in spirit, so we face our dire need for outside help. He remakes us boldly committed and grateful, knowing whom we have believed. He remakes us tender-hearted regarding the interests of others. As you become willing to "have other thoughts" of yourself than those that arise spontaneously, you initiate a torrent of other changes. The overthrow of your self-righteousness produces wonderfully different thoughts about Jesus Christ and other people.

But the soul's blind self-love resists this sort of change. The one activity that creates the truly human life feels harmful to us instinctively. What keeps us from loving and needing God with all that we are? Something in us doesn't want to face the Someone who insists on having the first and last say about our lives. Naturally, that something in us does not want to be seen for what it is. It is allergic to the truth about ourselves because we have an allergic reaction to "spiritual submission to God." We say *No, No, No* to life on God's terms, and we forfeit self-knowledge in the bargain.

"FOLLOW ME"

Yet the words of the personal Word and the power of the personal Spirit go patiently about the business of remaking us. God persistently teaches us to fear him, to trust him, to love him, and so, when we have ears to hear, we begin to serve him. To counsel others well, to seek wise counseling yourself, or to simply to be a Christian (in the rich Sibbes sense) all involve the same thing: a willingness to face up, to find mercy, and to change in this very particular way.

Only if you face up to your sin and your resistance to God can you see clearly and act gently, helping others to face up to themselves as well. The Bible calls this essential change dynamic by many names. Jesus says, "Become a disciple." In other words, sign on for life learning. A learner is committed to becoming different. Do your opinions, feelings, choices, and habits currently have the status of divine right? Is how you *are* a given, something you insist on? As soon as I'm willing to say "Not necessarily," I step off the death spiral and onto the learning curve.

Jesus says, "Follow me." To follow somebody else runs completely opposite to the self-will that characterizes what I do instinctively. Listening to him runs directly opposite to the opinions I obsessively think. *This* change dynamic will make you radically counter-intuitive. To follow somebody else runs flat opposite to the entitled self-assertiveness that western culture reinforces in us every day. *This* change dynamic will make you radically counter-cultural, while every alternative to "Follow me" is just another way of going with the flow.

Jesus says, "First take the log out of your own eye." Lightened of your sin's blindness, you begin to see yourself and to cling to the mercies of God. You will treat other people's failings more perceptively and gently. You will treat their troubles more generously. Every counseling model assumes some ideal of human functioning against which diagnoses are made and towards which the counseling process aims.² But only one counseling model on Earth proposes this particular ideal: to see yourself the way Jesus sees you, and to know Christ as the person he knows himself to be. Only the Word made flesh sees into our evil this deeply. Only the Lord of life aims us in the direction of what human life is meant to be: honest love for God and neighbor. Do you genuinely love God? Do you heartily consider the interests of others? How can you move in that direction? Those are the final exam questions in the school of life. Counseling that neglects these questions neglects reality.

THE WAR WITH YOURSELF

As you begin counseling any other person, you must be gripped by this vision. Without it, some species of self-deception will ultimately call the shots. Your finest insights and best intentions will short-circuit. None of us naturally approaches our troubles saying, "I must become different. *I* need help. Make *me* understand. Teach *me* simple trust, no matter what I face. Teach *me* to love other people. Teach *me* to respond well in every circumstance. Take away my grumbling, my anxiety, my pretense, my avoidance, my self-absorption. Forgive *me*. Change *me* by *your* mercy."

The Christian life is a lifelong "race of repentance,"[3] but we want to have arrived already. We don't like having to become different, but repentance is the Bible's word for "thorough, deep-seated, genuine change." It means turning from old ways to new. You wake up to find yourself living in God's universe, no longer sleepwalking through the universe of your desires and fears. A race of repentance calls for the ongoing reversal of our deepest instincts and opinions. You wake up again and again.

J. C. Ryle said that coming to vital Christian faith starts a lifelong quarrel inside a person: "You and sin must quarrel, if you and God are to be friends."[4] Imagine, I must quarrel with myself if I am to befriend God! To deal firmly with yourself is the hard way, the narrow way . . . and the only good way. Perhaps I should say it more strongly. To enter into yourself is the brutally wonderful, painstakingly delightful way. It sometimes feels like death, but always comes up life. The alternatives sometimes feel like life but always come up death.

Honest war with yourself comes paired with incomprehensible gifts. The peace of God passes all understanding, at the cost of all your fears! The love of God surpasses knowing, at the cost of every false love! Whatever you do, get this wisdom, this kingdom of God, this Christ! Nothing you could possibly desire compares. The cost is high: yourself. The reward is higher: no eye has seen, no ear has heard, no heart has conceived what God has prepared for those who love him.

Two Kinds of People

You counsel two kinds of people in principle. One kind will hear and embrace what Richard Sibbes stated so eloquently. Some hear immediately. Jesus can have his say and his way. Others hear more gradually. They may temporarily bristle at what is true, but sooner or later they listen. Even as they point a bitter finger at others or at God, or nurse narcotic self-pity, they listen to truth's reproof. Hearts soften and they eventually prove teachable. Sooner or later, this first kind of person is willing to come under subjection to God. He begins changing in the direction Jesus intends. If you are this kind of person, you may weave and stumble, but in roughly the right direction!

The other kind of person will not hear what Sibbes says. They are fundamentally closed to what the true God is all about. Perhaps they view God as "the errand boy to satisfy [their] wandering desires."[5] They might talk God-talk and be religiously active and have spiritual experiences . . . but they want something else out of it all. Or they might simply not care about God's point of view. Most non-hearers crave thinking well of themselves. They get angry when God insists we glorify him instead of serving our lust for self-esteem. Such people don't want to need Jesus. They want to be okay on their own. They want to be the hero of their own spiritual journey, not a small part in Jesus' story. To them, Sibbes's words are a depressing insult, not a doorway into unexpected joys.

Many cherished desires deafen people to the sanity of what Sibbes says – and so fulfill his prophecy. It's not easy to face yourself, to think differently about what you hold dear. People crave love, success, money and good health, fame and power, marriage and children, comfort, excitement, food and pleasure, independence and being right – and more. Does it make you angry that Jesus intends to revise your personal goals in order to "break your schemes for earthly joy"?[6] This second kind of person is fundamentally unteachable and will not make the daily U-turn that leads to life.

PROBING THE SOUL'S RESISTANCE

How does anyone muster up the courage to take any soul to task – including his or her own? How dare you assert to anyone that most of our lives are spent in fogs of self-deception? Interestingly, modern secular thought has spent a lot of time probing our resistance to knowing ourselves accurately. Tracing such "resistance" became a staple of serious thought about human nature in the nineteenth and early twentieth centuries. Nietzsche, Marx, and the psychodynamic psychologists (Freud, Jung, Adler, existentialists) all agreed that people resist looking in the mirror. They wanted to make honest persons of us all, whatever the blows to our pride and self-satisfaction.

The "masters of suspicion" were brilliant at seeing that we delude ourselves. But they could never agree on what we were avoiding or what the alternative is. They could never answer the crucial question, *What exactly is it that we're all so unwilling to see?* Is it perverse sexual impulses? Murderous hostilities? A cosmic dark side in our souls? A craving for power and superiority? A fear of death? The self-serving rationalization and hypocrisy of "civilized" existence? The inequities of wealth, power, and status? Great but godless thinkers disputed each other's theories; a Christian sees that each was partly right. All these things squirm within our souls. But all the theorists were ultimately wrong because an even darker cinder smolders inside us: "The hearts of the sons of men are full of evil, and insanity is in their hearts throughout their lives" (Eccl. 9:3). What is *that* referring to?

We human beings most fiercely resist seeing ourselves *as God sees us*, because we fiercely resist seeing God as he is. We don't want someone else to get final say – and we don't want to admit it. We don't want to need someone else to rescue us from ourselves. Compulsive unbelief and self-will (an *against*-God bias) are more ominous – and more interpersonal – than the psychological kinks of other theories. We compulsively rebel against the Person to whom we owe our lives. Our psychological kinks are wrongs done against the Person we are created to love. We are not first "psychologically" false. We are first interpersonally false, covenantally false, religiously false. We play false to ourselves *because* we play false to God and don't want to face up to it.

In another word, we sin. We don't want to know this. It's easier to admit sexual perversity, death wish, power drives, egotism, neediness, or class-consciousness than to admit sinfulness in the sight of God. Bad as they are, those other things are not the devastating blow that unglues us. This does.

You must approach counseling ministry with a keen awareness of this core choice in every human heart. The people who talk in any "counseling" conversation come with many different personal agendas. Few people begin with Sibbes's observation in mind! So start with yourself. Take your soul to task. You will then be better able to bring the hard and sweet words that others need, if they, too, are to let conscience have its full work.

3

HEARING THE MUSIC
OF THE GOSPEL

Frederick Faber's hymn, "Hark! Hark, my soul!" contains a wonderful line, "The music of the gospel leads us home."[1] Accurate self-knowledge leads us to need and know the God of love. Jesus Christ exactly maps onto our need.

We noted in Chapter 2 that the great secular thinkers could not agree on what it is that people so ardently avoid. Their blindness to God blinded them to the inner logic of the blindness they saw so clearly. They also disagreed about a second core question, *What can we do about the fact that we avoid self-knowledge?* Every theory proposes some way to make it right: Gain insight into personal history and psychodynamics. Undergo a re-education. Experience reparenting. Own your dark side. Make authentic choices. Raise your consciousness. Bring about the revolution of the proletariat. Or would you rather just keep taking your medications to take the edge off?

God's gaze, intentions and actions heal more deeply. Self-will cannot heal self-will. Unbelief cannot heal unbelief. Drugs cannot heal our allergy to self-knowledge. Only Jesus the Messiah can fix what has gone so wrong in us and around us. As discussed earlier, before we get tangled psychologically and socially, we have a relational problem with God. So the mercies of God come through a Person, who comes in person to restore peace. He alone touches deep enough to untangle the roots of everything else that troubles us.

FOUR FACETS OF CHRIST'S GRACE

Will you be able to counsel another? You must know the facts of life about people and the mercies of God in Christ. When Jesus opened the minds of his disciples to understand the Scriptures, he explained to them the gracious things concerning . . . himself. The Bible is *about* Jesus Christ, Savior and Lord. Therefore, counseling must be *about* Jesus Christ if it is to be true, biblical, and helpful. The grace you offer people has many facets. Let me mention four.

First, *God's past grace to sinners demonstrates that he is for us.* How do you know God is *for you*? He did not spare his own Son (Rom. 8:31-34a). This good news is not simply for giving birth to Christian life and experience. What Jesus *once did* continues to reshape what we do. For example, 2 Corinthians 5:14-15 identifies past grace as the power at work in transforming our present Christian life: *"The love of Christ* controls us, having concluded this, that *one died for all*, therefore all died; and *he died for all*, so that they who live might no longer live for themselves, but for him *who died* and *rose again on their behalf."*

Do you want to face yourself, change, and learn to live a new life? Past grace gives you the ability to fearlessly see yourself in the mirror of God's gaze, and gives you a reason to become different. You don't have to avoid looking or candy-coat your failures. You don't have to wallow in them either. Past grace never lets you forget that God the merciful Father is for you. Past grace keeps inviting you to trust him. It gives you confidence that today's sins will be freely forgiven too. It assures you that God will help you change now, and will someday finish what he has begun.

Second, *God's present grace to sinners demonstrates that he is with us and in us.* How do you know he is *with* you? The love of God has been poured into our hearts through the Holy Spirit who was given to us, by whom we cry out, "Abba, Father" (Rom. 5:5, 8:15). The good news is not simply what happened long ago and far away. What Jesus *now does* reshapes what we do. For example, Ephesians bases the transformational power of the Christian life on the oft-repeated promise of power and presence now: "the surpassing greatness of *his power* toward us who believe, in accordance with the *working* of the *strength* of *his might* . . . *strengthened with power* through *his Spirit in the inner man*, so that *Christ may dwell in your hearts* through faith . . . *him who is able to do* far more abundantly beyond all that we ask or think, according to *the power that works within* us . . . Be *strong in the Lord and in the strength of his might*." God is present with us and works powerfully in us. Our Father gives wisdom for the asking. The Holy Spirit comes for the asking. Good gifts are for the asking. The Bible repeatedly invites us to need, ask, receive, and live on present grace. Would you die to yourself and live a new life? Present grace gives you the confidence to seek help, to question those old felt needs, desires, opinions, and lifestyles, to put to death what is not beautiful. Present grace nourishes faith working through love.

Third, *God's future grace to sinners demonstrates that he will come to us*. How do you know that he will come for you, that he will make right all the wrongs that rise up within you? "We know that when he appears, we will be like him, because we will see him just as he is" (1 John 3:2). The good news is not simply past and present. What Jesus *will do* reshapes what we do. For example, 1 Peter bases the transformational power of the Christian life now on what will happen in the future. "Fix your hope completely on the grace to be brought to you at the revelation of Jesus Christ. As obedient children, do not be conformed to the former lusts which were yours in your ignorance" (1:13-14). How will you hang in over the long haul, growing wiser until the end? Future grace beckons you.

Fourth, *God's past, present, and future grace to sufferers demonstrates that he hears the cry of the afflicted*. Grace is not only a mercy to sinners, but a mercy to sufferers. Jesus dies for the wicked; he also defends the innocent, feeds the hungry, gives refuge to the broken, and heals the sick. How do you know that you are safe? "Moses said to God, 'Who am I, that I should go to Pharaoh?' . . . And [the LORD] said, 'Certainly I will be with you'" (Ex. 3:11-12). At the center of the Christian life is our need and God's protection. In the past, he showed such mercies, in part to give us hope today (1 Cor. 10:11; Rom. 15:4).

Right now he helps, comforts, heals, and encourages. Someday he will act decisively to remove all heartache and bring joy to pass (Rev. 20:4). His mercies to the broken change the way you face whatever afflicts you.

THE GOSPEL'S PLACE IN COUNSELING

What is the place of Christ's good news in biblical counseling? That is rather like asking, "What is the place of water and carbon in human physiology?" The gospel of Jesus is the fundamental stuff of biblical counseling. Counseling that lacks Jesus, however skillful, is not wise. Counseling based on what God does and says will itself be composed of grace. Why do people sometimes wonder whether grace is central to biblical counseling? Here are three reasons.

A Narrow Perspective

First, for many people the Bible functions within a narrow scope. It gives a religious formula to "get people saved" and then tells them what to do morally: doctrine, conversion experience, and moral values. From that perspective, all a biblical counselor might say to people is, "Here's how to accept Christ so that you'll go to heaven. Now, until that day, here are the rules." But such moralizing and spiritualizing flies against the Bible's real call. God never tacks willpower and self-effort onto grace. His words are about all of life, not some religious sector.

What happens as the scope and relevance of your Bible expands? God's self-revelation becomes the environment you live in. His promises become the food you live on. God's commands become the life you live out. Biblical counseling worthy of the name is a ministry of God's own power in the gospel, changing people inwardly and outwardly.

Equating Obedience with Moralism

Here is a second reason some people wonder about the place of grace in biblical counseling: Counseling that thinks biblically aims for practical obedience. Faith must work through love. Many people think that emphasizing obedience to God's commands equates with moralism. But when *God* calls for our obedience and a holy life, does that mean he is ignoring or contradicting the grace of his own gospel? May it never be!

Free grace – past, present, and future – is effective grace. It intends to change us from our sins in the midst of our sufferings. The gracious Master, who learned obedience through what he suffered, remakes disciples who become like him. "In his image" is the formal phrase for becoming more honest, constructive, purposeful, and loving.

What is the alternative to obedience and holiness of life? It is no treat to be forgiven adultery, and yet remain adulterous. It is no glory to God to forgive anger, and yet leave a person irritable, explosive, and self-righteous. It is no honor to the gospel if anxiety can be forgiven, yet someone remains a nervous wreck. It is no advance for God's kingdom to forgive self-centered people, if they do not learn how to consider the interests of others. It does no good to the world or the church if a forgiven war-maker does not learn how to become a practical peacemaker. Grace takes a lazy, selfish, thieving person, and pushes him in the direction of becoming hard-working and generous. God will remake a liar into an honest man and a shrewish complainer into a kind, constructive woman.

These are long journeys, but the direction of grace is towards obedience to God's law of love. None of these changes mean perfection until Jesus returns. You will always need mercies to be renewed every morning. But there is substantial healing amid the ongoing struggle. It isn't always dramatic. Small choices count. But the Spirit will produce his fruit in us, and biblical counseling serves such practical changes.

Failures in Counseling

The third reason some people wonder about the place of grace in biblical counseling is that we as biblical counselors fall far short of what we aspire to. We profess to be biblical, but our failings – in counsel and manner, in doctrine and life – contradict what we profess and intend. Aspiration outstrips attainment. When I am clumsy or ignorant, harsh or moralistic, mystical or preachy, fearful or confused, grace gets called into question. What biblical counselor has not failed while attempting to serve others the whole counsel of God?

The solution is not to give up on "biblical counseling." That's like giving up on automobiles because your car broke down. If we are to counsel the way the Bible teaches, then we always need to become more biblical, more full of effective grace and truth. The Lord will reveal our shortcomings. He will make us need the wisdom he gives without reproach.

Grace-full Methods

As we listen, the Bible equips us to counsel the truth in God's penetrating way. Jesus faced people with themselves (by facing them with himself). And he did so in love, to enlighten, to forgive, and to set free – not to condemn. Biblical counseling carries the gracious message of a gracious Savior. Counselors faithful to that message and Savior must embody the methods that correspond to the message.

- An honest and gentle curiosity probes the reality of another's life.
- Loving candor speaks up truly, frankly, personally, and helpfully.
- Humility is willing to learn, to admit ignorance and fault.
- Boldness does and says what is needed.
- Dependency upon God prays through one's own sins and troubles as the context for speaking into others'.
- Wisdom takes a person's welfare to heart, and considers timing, tone of voice, choice of words, the needs of this moment.
- Gentleness breathes a respectful tenderheartedness for people in their struggles.
- Authority presents the words and calling of God himself, his promises and his commands.
- Kindness demonstrates constructive intention.
- Realism does not shrink from the ugly, painful, and evil.
- Persistence holds on, willing to come back to what matters.
- Courage is not intimidated, distracted, or driven to please.

- Flexibility adapts to the ever-changing conditions of people's lives.
- Generosity is self-giving, willing to enter another's sins and sorrows, willing to make his struggles and concerns one's own.
- Shepherdly pursuit initiates relationship, rather than waiting for those who ask for help.
- Patience is the first word on love for good reason, because lives are always flawed, troubles never cease, and no one's life is ever all better.

The Bible is about all this. It equips us as counselors to minister the whole counsel of God in Christ's way of speaking and acting. Therefore, biblical counseling must also be *about* equipping counselors to minister in love.

You are not simply bringing a better theory about persons and the change process. When you counsel, you are representing, incarnating, and bringing a living Redeemer to people who need him. Every person on earth will bow before Jesus eventually, in either joy or woe. You are working for the joy of those you counsel. You must bring Christ himself, if you are serving the purposes of the Holy Spirit and the Word. Such counseling merits the label Christian.

The place of grace? Biblical counseling is the ministry of God's grace to individuals, just as biblical preaching is the ministry of God's grace to crowds. Grace is the only context in which to take any soul to task.

4 How Healthy is Your Preparation?

A student once asked me, "How do you prepare for a counseling session? Why do you prepare in the ways you do?" Those are good questions. They drew me to consider the difference between being well-prepared and ill-prepared. Here's what happens when I'm doing it right.

First, I follow through on my commitments. If I said I'd make a phone call, I do it. If I planned to write the person a letter, or design a personalized homework assignment, or copy an article, I get it done. If I intended to seek advice from another counselor, I pursue it. Tangible love plays a significant role in pastoral progress. It affects me, for one thing. I find that when I have acted to love someone, I care more in subsequent interactions. I probe more carefully. I listen better. My counsel is warmer and more personal.

It also affects the other person. He experiences the immediate blessing of my action, and also observes a small model of the sorts of changes God is typically working in *his* life. Why do things for people? How can we *not* do such things if Christian "counseling" is simply part of making disciples of Christ – and Christ is making me a disciple, too? Such actions simply express what it means to be Christ's people.

Second, I check out my own attitudes and life. If I'm bitter, anxious, grumpy, fearful, or presumptuous, I deal with it. Sometimes my sin may relate to the person I'll be counseling. I might be viewing the upcoming meeting as "too hard," feeling intimidated or anxious. Perhaps I recognize that I'll be tempted to play it safe rather than risk speaking the truth in love. Perhaps I realize that I'm tempted to dislike someone, and so to become harsh or impatient. Or I might be viewing the meeting as "too easy," feeling overly confident and in control. At such times, I'm tempted not to prepare, not to pray for God to work, not to care intensely, but to simply go through the motions.

Sometimes my sin or struggle pertains to another part of my life. Perhaps I'm fretting about money or unfinished tasks; maybe I haven't resolved a spat with my wife. Biblical counseling takes its own medicine first, to the praise of God's grace. I find that the state of my own faith, repentance, and obedience is the single most significant factor affecting the counseling I do. When I'm a changing person, I'm better able to help others become the same.

Third, I read and study the Bible. I do this extensively (through the Bible each year) and intensively (focusing in on particular passages). Recently, Titus, Psalms, and Ephesians have been my companions for months at a time. Why? Because I need the same radical reorientation as those to whom I minister. When I'm thinking straight, counseling bears sweet fruit.

Fourth, I think hard about those with whom I'll meet. I go over notes, especially from the previous meeting. I often take extensive notes either during or after meeting with someone. I go back through these with a yellow highlighter. I'm looking for – and praying to understand – what I call the "watershed issues." Where is this person facing a significant choice to live out either the "former manner of life" or a new life of specific faith and love? God's grace is at work in people, teaching us to say No to our natural darkness and selfishness, and to say Yes to the light (Titus 2:11-15; Eph. 4:17-5:10). I'll ponder the issues on which the previous conversation turned. Where did we get to? Where does this person typically get stuck in life? If our previous session was on target, then identifying the watershed issue usually led to setting some goals together:

a choice to embrace the truth in faith, a commitment to act in obedience. I'll want to follow up on that, to see what has been done with counsel.

My concern to identify watershed issues arises from several foundational truths. Our Father is a vinedresser who prunes those he loves (John 15:1-2). He is a father who raises children intentionally, with specific goals in mind (Heb. 12:5-6). Ministry relies on this sovereign and gracious providence. A person's struggles typically organize around key themes, and when I counsel, I want to offer new and specific wisdom to replace my counselee's "characteristic flesh." As I know a person truly, I get to see the particular form of his or her struggle to believe and obey.

Fifth, I pray for each person, asking God to work. Obviously, people don't change because they "go to counseling." They change significantly because God works in them and they work out his call: "Work out your salvation . . . for it is God who is at work in you, both to will and to work for his good pleasure" (Phil. 2:12-13). So I ask the Holy Spirit to bring to my counselee a conviction of the truth about himself and about the One who is full of grace and truth.

I pray for myself, also. I need all the requisites of pastoral care: wisdom, clarity, courage, a breadth and depth of biblical knowledge. I need many abilities: to listen hard and well, to enter the person's world, to apply Scripture, to speak the word that builds up and gives grace, to communicate love, to be honest, to get practical, to "be patient with them all." I ask my family and coworkers to pray both for me and for those I counsel.

Sixth, I set a rough agenda for our meeting. It might be as open-ended as finding out what's really going on. It might be as specific as "teach and role-play reconciliation principles," or "check out whether they are still avoiding each other," or "Psalm 31: the refuge that's an alternative to self-pity, fear, anger, and escapism." Sometimes my agenda includes a specific exhortation to myself. "You spoke too quickly last time; think for five more seconds before you speak." Or, "You were vague and minced words; just say it clearly and boldly." Or, "Be more cheerful and humorous." Or, "Be more serious; humor almost offended last week."

Biblical counselors differ on how detailed their agenda is and how consistently they intend to stick to it. Some take a rather programmatic approach to discipleship. I do this sometimes, but I lean towards the more flexible end of the spectrum. I think the strengths of tightly structured counseling emerge with counselees who are either highly committed to change or who are pointedly rebellious in a highhanded way. In the broad middle, I've found that it's better to let the specific agenda emerge in the give-and-take of an honest relationship. I like to look for what's happening – "What's hot off the press?" I may set an open-ended Titus 2:11-15 agenda and see what emerges. Usually the watershed issues play out afresh, and face-to-face ministry takes on vibrancy and immediacy. The person has reacted to events of the day or week past. The person is reacting to things happening right now. The person is already reacting to events of the day or week ahead. Counseling becomes immediately relevant.

Many of the greatest joys of face-to-face ministry emerge amid the unpredictability of human reactions, in the need of the moment, in the challenge of winning a person whose commitment to change is fickle, in disarming a person whose anger and defensiveness fill the room, in the delicate task of encouraging the faint-hearted, in hearing some painful secret that had never been voiced before, in witnessing acts of courageous faith and godliness. I think structured programs have their place, and perhaps the situation in which you typically counsel is one that highlights the strengths. But let me argue a biblical rationale for approaching counseling with a more open-ended agenda: I'm impressed by the wondrous flexibility manifested by Scripture itself. No two prophets, no two psalms, no two gospels (indeed, no two interactions between Jesus and his hearers), no two apostolic letters are quite the same. God's unified truth gets communicated in diverse ways, tailored to the diverse needs of audience and situation. Biblical counseling should also prize freshness and flexibility, insight and creativity.

Seventh, I often review basic principles of counseling to orient myself. I hadn't thought about the fact that I did this until my student posed her question. Here are some of the reminders posted in the vicinity of my desk.

- "How can even this situation prove redemptive?" If I never lose hope in Christ's gracious control and redemptive agenda, I will be able to communicate the same to those I counsel.
- "Most people don't know that their biggest problem is not 'out there' in the world; it's 'in here' in their own heart." Always move the agenda towards the person sitting in front of me.
- "Love. Know. Speak. Do." Counselors care, probe, speak Ephesians 4:15 and 4:29 truth, and help people make concrete changes. Am I covering all the bases? Am I on the right base now?
- "Whatever you do in word or deed, do all in the name of the Lord Jesus, giving thanks through him to God the Father" (Col. 3:17). I am a servant called to be faithful and full of faith, not a technician called to fix things.
- "Get to specifics. After all the talking is done, what are you going to do about your watershed issue this week?" Change happens in the details, in the step-step-step of your walk. Effective counseling moves towards substantive change.
- "This life, therefore, is not righteousness but growth in righteousness . . . . We are not yet what we shall be, but we are growing toward it." As this quote from Luther attests, small changes accumulate; a glimpse of final glory.
- "Counseling – no magic, no technique, no sure cure." Biblical counseling is simply the way of speaking wisely with moral decision-makers who will trust and obey either lies or truth.

I need reminding. Otherwise the sinful inertia of my own tendencies may hijack the ministry goals set by the great Shepherd of the sheep.

Eighth, I do things that orient me to the ministry task. This, too, I'd never really thought about before my questioner piped up. I might take a walk outside – to take a few deep breaths, to let my eyes drink in patterns of cloud and tree, to smell and feel the wind. A walk outside reminds me that God's world is much bigger than my office. That site where problems can loom large is situated in a universe whose God of grace looms larger.

Sometimes I'll sit for a few minutes in the chairs in which those I counsel will soon be seated. I try to reflect on what it's like to be on that side of the room and on that side of the conversation. I can never actually feel what another person's life is like: "The heart knows its own bitterness, and a stranger does not share its joy" (Prov. 14:10). But sitting in the chair helps me realize that a person bears these sorrows and struggles with these sins. I will counsel people with problems, not problems with people somehow attached.

Sometimes I'll eat dinner – and enjoy it in a quiet half hour. I suppose that even enjoying dinner expresses, in its own way, a significant part of how to prepare for the tasks of counseling! The God whose goodness provides daily bread, who gives all things richly to enjoy, will surely also give wisdom to his children. When all is said and done, the kingdom is his. That is a fountain of comfort and peace amid the difficulties of the work.

Prepare well!

5 WHAT QUESTIONS DO YOU ASK?

All vital ministry of Word and Spirit arises at an intersection: Truth meets truth. Divine Redeemer meets honest human need. So when people meet for discipleship or pastoral counseling, the key elements of that more profound meeting must get on the table. Something is at stake *today*, between God and every one of his creatures, however consciously faithful or blindly disobedient we are. This being so, two key questions must weave through all that is said and done in discipleship.

First, what is this person facing in life? To put it more pointedly, what is *your* greatest struggle and need *right now*? Where will you face *today's* crucial choices? In that moment, in that situation, what will you do? How will you treat people? What will you believe? Where will you place (or misplace) your trust? What will you want? How will you react in that circumstance? These questions look for the significant, decisive choices in a person's everyday life: "When you face that situation, which way will you turn?"

Second, what does the Lord say that speaks directly into what you are facing? Who is he? What is he doing? What does he promise? What does he will? And what does he call you to believe, need, trust, hope, and obey? These questions explore a person's current perceptions of the God who is there. Is what God says and does immediately relevant or basically irrelevant?

Both questions help us to work on the things that count. Ministry is always helping people make connections they haven't been making. It's always reinterpreting what's going on, identifying redemptive opportunities in what seem like the same old ruts. It traces out previously unseen practical implications of life in Christ. It's always remaking minds, hearts, and lifestyles that are still misshapen. These questions will help you to say the timely, significant, and appropriate words that encourage such a discipling of lives.

UNDERSTANDING THE PERSON

The first question helps us grasp the environment (providentially arranged by the Vinedresser) in which growth (or hardening) takes place daily. It makes discipleship relevant. Occasionally there is a big issue, a major choice of life direction. But usually the watershed moments occur in the tiny choices of life: the words we say or don't say; the attitudes we adopt or resist; the tasks we pick up or neglect; the ways we love or ignore another; our reaction to some typical trouble. If love is the Spirit's fruit, we need him right then and there.

The second question helps us grasp what this person does (or does not) understand about God and how he meets us. It enables discipleship to build on what someone already knows. (But how easily we forget, get distracted, or turn willfully away!) You can then judiciously add what someone doesn't yet know that makes a difference. Often people we disciple already know significant truth, but they don't know it in a way that changes their lives. Discipleship does the hard work of kneading what is true into how we actually live.

You will ask these two questions in a hundred different ways. They are things that you the discipler must continually be asking of everything you see and hear, whether or not you actually pose these questions aloud. You are looking for the significant real-time turning points – today, this week, during this season of this person's life. You are looking for the places where you can say to another, "*Here* is where you need *this* grace and truth." I'll often say to someone, "The Vinedresser uses pruning shears, not a chain saw. He's not going to work on everything all at once. He's not going to make you face every kind of trouble right now. He's not going to teach you everything about himself. But *something* about who he is and what he says to you can make a decisive difference in *some* challenge you are facing right now." In discipling another, I am doing nothing more than pursuing the same line of questioning and reasoning that I need myself. God meets you – and me – exactly where we are. That's all these questions are about.

I suspect that most of our discipleship efforts do better at teaching people basic theology, Bible knowledge, Christian ethics, God's promises, ministry techniques, and the disciplines of grace than they do at asking the questions that make all those teachings sparkle with relevance. Perhaps that's why I've found these questions to be so fruitful. They help me to better understand the people God has called me to serve (and understand myself as well). They help others to better understand how God meets them in real life (even as they help me).

UNDERSTANDING THE WORD

It is also significant that these two questions help you to understand Scripture. Think about that for a minute. You should ask the same things of the Bible that you ask of people. Why not? The Bible is about people, and troubles, and mercies, and choices, and struggles, and hope. So ask of Scripture, What were those people facing back then? What did God choose to reveal to them? Today's specific situations and choices are never exactly the same, but there are always common themes. And though our saving God never works in exactly the same way twice, he is the same yesterday, today, and forever.

These two questions help you to get a feel for how Scripture operates. The Word is not a textbook of normative and propositional truths. It does not operate like a systematic theology text, dense with abstracted propositions logically arranged. And it is not a treasury of verse-sized proof-texts. A topical study using a concordance is often not the best way to understand something biblically. The Bible is not a how-to book, a self-help book, or an inspirational reading. Scripture does not work like a handbook full of abstracted principles, advice, steps, sayings, and anecdotes. Instead, the Word of God reveals God's person, promises, ways, and will on the stage and in the story of real human lives. Our two questions attune us to that. In our counseling ministry, we should seek to work in much the same way that Scripture works. We are discipling the same kinds of people who originally received any particular chunk of the Word. So let's get the living God into the daily watershed moments! Let me summarize, and then illustrate.

At every turn, the Word of God shows people facing particular challenges and choices. Amid the troubles and opportunities of their lives, they are tempted to believe particular lies, to choose particular wrongs, and to live in ways that are ugly, perverse, and complicated. This is our Question 1.

Scripture also shows us the Lord of life, the true and living God who enters the human condition redemptively, making wrongs right, speaking wisdom that we need. This is our Question 2.

And, amid all the troubles and opportunities, Scripture shows some people believing what is true, choosing what is good, and living in ways that are simply beautiful – people after God's own heart. They need, seek, and turn to the Lord. Supremely, we witness the true Man after God's own heart, that bright Lord, Word made flesh, living with us, touched by our weakness, full of grace, truth and glory, loving God and neighbor. This is the goal of our discipleship.

AN EXAMPLE FROM THE PSALMS

Consider a simple example of how Scripture disciples us amid what we face. Has anyone ever faced a threat situation more wonderfully and honestly?

> Be gracious to me, O God, be gracious to me,
> For my soul takes refuge in you,
> And in the shadow of your wings I will take refuge
> Until destruction passes by.
> I will cry to God Most High,
> To God who accomplishes all things for me.
> He will send from heaven and save me.

He reproaches him who tramples upon me.
God will send forth his lovingkindness and his truth.

(Ps. 57:1-3)

Notice all the active verbs. They describe the God I honestly need (Question 2 again). Are those you disciple learning such a straight-on relationship with this God?

Notice how the psalm proceeds. A man vividly portrays his experience facing danger, and he intends to evoke that experience in you, connecting to what you face. Imagine yourself feeling threatened by people with destructive intentions . . . trampled and run over . . . surrounded by lions . . . lying helpless on the ground amid fire-breathing predators . . . assaulted by violent killers whose mouths are spears, arrows, and swords . . . trapped by people out to get you, who spread a net and dig a pit in order to catch you (vv. 3, 4, 6).

In short, terrorists are in your town. But that's just the extreme version of everyday life in the human jungle. Gossips and backbiters talk it up in your workplace. Factions spring up in your church. Family members manipulate, nag, lie, scheme, and gang up on you to get their way. That other driver, gripped by road rage, gestures obscenities at you.

So what are *you* facing today? Anything that threatens you? (Question 1 again.) The psalm makes the experience of danger chillingly specific, but it leaves specific circumstances undefined. That invites disciples to insert their own details.

Notice further, amid this disturbing and difficult experience, the astonishing centerpiece of the psalm: "Be exalted above the heavens, O God. Let your glory be above all the earth" (v. 5). It is a wonder. Here is the living faith towards which true discipleship aims. Pointedly placed right in the midst of troubles, this is a whole different way of seeing things and responding. These sentences are the pivot around which everything in the psalm turns. The people you disciple don't yet think this way very often. You and I don't think this way very often. People who feel threatened usually react with fear, retaliation, or escapism. They forget the exalted One. Discipleship aims to help such people remember.

And finally, has anyone ever expressed the essence of joy more wonderfully and honestly than this?

My heart is steadfast, O God, my heart is steadfast;
I will sing, yes, I will sing praises!
Awake, my glory!
Awake, harp and lyre!
I will awaken the dawn.
I will give thanks to you, O Lord, among the peoples;
I will sing praises to you among the nations.
For your lovingkindness is great to the heavens
And your truth to the clouds.
Be exalted above the heavens, O God;
Let your glory be above all the earth. (Ps. 57:7-11)

Here on the stage of real-time troubles and choices, we have witnessed the two chief modes of faith in operation: need and gladness. We have seen a disciple, an image bearer, a man after God's heart, in the midst of his thinking, feeling, and acting.

Such living faith is the fountainhead of the final goal of our discipleship: all the practicalities and necessities of obedience to God, love, service, courage, holy resistance to evil, and mercy. Our discipleship aims for these beautiful and practical actions on the stage of real life. Psalm 57 is only a short video clip of the vertical dimension operating amid life's troubles. But it sets up the horizontal dimension we see in Ephesians 4, 1 Corinthians 13, Romans 12, 1 Peter, Luke 6:21-49, and the rest of the Lord's ethic of practical love operating amid hardships.

This is the payoff. These details of small, constructive, and otherwise inexplicable obediences are the payoff. Faith works through love. These are the how-tos of forgiveness transacted, of constructive choices, of good communication, of vigorous peacemaking, of wise decision making, of financial steward-ship, and all the rest. This is "the image of Christ" working into a disciple's heart and working out into a disciple's walk.

These two simple questions – What are you facing? How does the Lord connect? – express the core agenda of our disci-pleship. They set up the call to explicit faith and explicit love.

6 THINK GLOBALLY, ACT LOCALLY

You know the problem well.

On the one hand, our Lord gives us the living words of Scripture, so full of glory and good sense. On the other hand, you have a living person sitting in front of you, a never-to-be-repeated mosaic of troubles and wonders. And between the two, there is a fundamental disconnect.

The Word is alive with the love of God in Christ Jesus. He invades our darkness and his words vividly portray the human struggle. The wise will of God is realistic and relevant, as God shows himself operating in the midst of the worst and best of life and all the muddling in the middle. Scripture is timely, adapted to the varied conditions and experiences of real people, because God is a timely Redeemer.

But this person is a dark tangle. Other voices besides God's configure his reality. He doesn't get it and he's going astray – "ignorant and wayward" in the pithy words of Hebrews 5:2. Therefore you "deal gently." You pick your way through confusion, distortion, good intentions gone bad, good perceptions gone sour, disillusioned hopes, petty conceits next door to amazingly generous acts, and the quiet grind of anguish and loneliness. What goes on inside this person is too often malignant, graceless, frightened, sordid, or depressing. Perhaps even when he says the right words, they sound simplistic or shallow, sanctimonious or even brutal. Those words of life ought to be meaningful, but they seem void of nutritional content.

This disconnect is the stuff of ministry. The Redeemer says

and does one story; how we live is another. So how do you bring truth to life? How do you apply the Word of God? How does his truth inform our honesty, and our honesty engage his truth?

Ministry is hard when you grope to bridge that disconnect with someone, when the call to wise love collides with a person's willfulness or fear. Perhaps you get discouraged or disillusioned. Sometimes we forget that there are *two* counselors talking in every human conversation, and often the "counselee" is the more persuasive and skilled counselor! He, after all, lives his story from the inside. You are the stranger exploring strange lands. Counselors are extremely vulnerable to disinformation: things that are true enough but steadily misleading. Even if you keep your wits about you, you feel your powerlessness in the face of an uncanny force field. The sufferer remains comfortless. These disconnects occur *exactly* where help is most needed.

This, by the way, is not only a counseling problem, but also a how-to-live-your-life problem. In technical terms, it is *the* hermeneutical problem. How do you connect "far horizon" (interpreting Scripture) with "near horizon" (interpreting a life here and now)? How do you do that double exegesis – of both Word and person – from which ministry arises? After all, our Bibles portray people who lived way over there and way back then. Their lives revealed the redemptive words and demonstrated the redeeming works. But how do the here-and-now stories connect to God's long ago stories?

A TWO-BIT ANSWER TO THE MILLION DOLLAR QUESTION

This chapter will consider one small but important part of the answer. Learning this has made a huge impact on how I live and counsel. In a nutshell, it is this: *Connect one bit of Scripture to one bit of life.* Always ask two questions of yourself and others: *What is your current struggle? What about God in Christ connects to this?*

What is your struggle? You might be facing troubles (James 1:2). You might be sinning, doing troublesome things (James 3:16). Usually it's a tangle of both. God talks about both of these things. How does the Savior enter these struggles? What does he say? How does he help? What will he change?

Perhaps you've seen the ecology-minded bumper sticker that says, "Think globally. Act locally." Keep the big picture in view and then do something immediately constructive. The same principle operates in counseling. Keep the big picture in view, then act on some detail. Get the whole Story on God. Get the whole story on this person. Then apply one relevant thing from our Redeemer to one significant scene in this person's story. Bring one bit of Bible to one bit of life. Charles Spurgeon put the principle in his inimitable way:

> One bit of Bible prayed over, and bedewed with the Spirit, and made alive, though it be only a short sentence of six words, will profit you more than a hundred chapters without the Spirit.[1]

One bit of Bible, bedewed with the Spirit, comes to life in one bit of life! Ministry, like life, goes one step at a time.

Apply this first to your own life. The best advice I ever got on preaching was this: "Live your message for a week, a month, a lifetime. Then aim low. You're sure to hit something." The same thing applies to would-be counselors. What is your current struggle? How does God in Christ connect to you in this? You *can* give away what you are being given. When you are learning kindness from your Savior, you will be able to teach unkind people. When you are learning to endure suffering well, you will be able to reach sufferers. It is the same with any other radiancy of the Spirit: clarity, courage, humility, patience, joy, wisdom, gratitude, mercy, teachability, generosity, honesty.

Richard Baxter graphically named the alternative: "I confess I must speak it by lamentable experience, that I publish to my flock the distempers of my own soul. When I let my heart go cold, my preaching is cold; and when it is confused, my preaching is confused."[2] As with preaching, so with counseling. In fact, the impact for good or ill occurs more instantaneously in counseling. People come vulnerable; their struggles out on the table. You don't have the luxury of planning even the next sentence to come out of your mouth. You immediately reveal what is in your soul by the questions you ask (or don't ask), by how you listen (or fail to), by the interpretations you offer (or don't even think to offer), by the advice you give (or can't give), by the attitude you take towards people, problems, and people with problems.

THREE ESSENTIAL THINGS

Offering one timely passage does three essential things.

It orients the person to his life. It lays out to the person the moral landscape within which he lives: "The unfolding of your words gives light" (Ps. 119:132). If someone gets lost in dark woods, a good map and the light of dawn are extremely helpful! They don't actually get him anywhere, but they help him to see where he's gotten and where he needs to get. It must be simple and concrete – something riveted to real life. Theological generalities and intricacies don't do the job. General truths about your tendencies, patterns, and themes in your personal history don't change you either. You must be able to identify where your particular current struggle lies, what it means, what exactly is at stake, and where to go. Where is the firefight between good and evil today? You must be able to trace the difference between truth and lies, hope and illusion, insight and self-deception, true need and wild desires, living faith and functional godlessness. Where do you need God's redemption and help? When you are disoriented in your current struggle, you don't know even your choices. When your way is deep darkness, you don't know what makes you stumble. The right bit of Scripture reorients you.

A timely passage brings Christ's grace and truth. Something that God is, says, and does must invade your struggles to teach and master you. What about God in Christ do you need today? The map-giver personally guides you through the dark woods. You need help, and the LORD is a very present help in trouble. You can't make it without grace to help in your time of need. The people you counsel can't either.

The first beatitude on essential poverty, need, and weakness comes first for a reason: We need what God gives. We need our Father to give the Holy Spirit to us, so that Christ dwells in our hearts by faith, and so that the love of God is poured out within us right when the heat is on. Augustine summarized the immediacy of grace this way: "Give what you command and command what you will." Some part of the good news of the Lord's redemptive purposes, will, and promise is absolutely necessary – right now.

The Bible models how ministry and life focus on one thing at a time. A good theology book rightly asks, Who is God? and goes on to fill 400 pages with truths. But Psalm 121 cries out, "Where does my help come from?", and seizes on one necessary thing: "The LORD keeps me."

A timely passage invites change. In the Bible's vivid picture, we "turn" to our Father, Savior, and Comforter. He works in us toward one goal: change. The central dynamic of the Christian life has this FROM . . . TO . . . movement. "Repentance is not merely the start of the Christian life; it is the Christian life."[3] Faith does new transactions and conversations with God. Love does new actions and choices on the stage of life. When God calls, you listen. When he promises, you trust and talk back to him in your need. When he loves, you love. When he commands, you obey. You aim your life in a new direction by the power of the Holy Spirit. In every case, you turn.

These are the purposes of the whole Bible, the whole mission of our Redeemer. When you get to know a person well, you know both the panorama and the details. But biblical change walks out in the details.

The patterns, themes, and tendencies of our lives are what we see when, figuratively, we view our lives from the observation deck of the Empire State Building. From one hundred floors up, Manhattan and the Hudson River spread serenely before you. But the action and noise of life happens at the corner of Fifth Avenue and 34th Street, and when we take the Lincoln Tunnel home to Hoboken. The big stories of our lives are worked out in a running series of small scenes. This is how

God has made it to be, but this is something that counselors and preachers often don't understand.

When you counsel (or preach) in great and good generalities, people will nod, but they rarely change. Jesus works for a turn-the-world-upside-down reorientation and redirection. Ministry needs to know the big picture, but it really gets involved in the rush hour traffic. Change takes place in the watershed moments and decisive incidents of everyday life.

What does this look like when you're actually talking with someone? What does it mean you should give a person to take into the week ahead?

A CASE STUDY

Teri gets easily intimidated in social situations. She's shy, insecure, and tongue-tied, fearing disapproval and rejection by others. To avoid social pain, she's generally overly compliant as she negotiates her way through life. Teri gets cowed by her Mom, manipulated by her boyfriend, bullied by her boss, and exploited by coworkers.

Yet Teri is very aware of her tendencies, insightful about others, and quite witty when she opens up. She knows that when her boyfriend pressures her for sex, his desire to win sex and her desire to win approval lead to a "win-win" that ultimately means she loses. Teri makes herself an inconspicuous, agreeable chameleon in her small group at church. She's afraid to be honest even when she talks with you, afraid to really express how deeply she struggles with bitterness, anxiety, despair, loneliness, jealousy, guilt, and fantasy. After all, you're yet another person whose approval can be won or lost.

Teri is skilled at reading people, good at telling them what they want to hear, good at doing what they want her to do. She can easily feed you a steady and plausible stream of disinformation. The dark jungle of her inner world and the bland civility of her outer manner express an obsessive people-pleasing.

Some of the same themes play out in her relationship with God. Since a people pleaser lives for "my achievement in the eyes of others," God is yet another person that Teri is nervous about pleasing. Deep down, she's afraid of failing and being rejected by him. Her Christianity is dutiful, joyless, formal, and haunted. She wears the clumsy armor of Christianity, not the lively weaponry of God. Her fear is not a wide-awake, liberating fear of the Lord; it's a furtive fearfulness about a capricious god who offers no gospel. She treats God with the same compliant superficiality that characterizes other relationships.

It's easy to describe Teri's typical *modus operandi*, isn't it? But what's really going on inside Teri? Why is she like this?

WHAT'S INSIDE TERI?

First, it is relevant that Teri lives in a world full of people who are judgmental, manipulative, opinionated, and predatory. We live among sinners. It's difficult to live among people who pursue self-interest first and foremost, banishing the real God from their universe. Teri lives out her life amid significant "trials and temptations," and these pressures typically bring out the worst in her. The wrongs of others easily lead her into similar evils. If her boyfriend pressures her to sleep with him, what will she do? The wrongs of others too easily tempt her to retaliate with evil for evil. If her boyfriend drops her, will she be consumed with hatred, vengeful fantasies, and suicidal shame? But this is precisely where Christ and Scripture operate. Her sufferings are the God-arranged context within which the Holy Spirit is bent on remaking her. He aims to teach her to return good for evil, with courageous, loving honesty, sexual purity, a purposeful life, and forgiveness received and given.

Second, Teri's drift in core loyalties gets expressed in her behavior, thoughts, and emotions. "Prone to wander, Lord, I feel it, prone to leave the God I love." Her preoccupation with the opinions of others and her felt need for their approval drown out any concern for the Lord's opinion and any sense of need for *his* approval and mercy. This unholy preoccupation hijacks her trust in his mercies. She is deaf to his call to honesty and constructive action in relationships. The Bible calls her problem "fear of man." Teri's compulsive anti-repentance and anti-faith are a typically human sin: turning *from* God *to* other people's opinions and desires. Her anxiety, bitterness, immorality, and the rest arise from that source.

Third, God also names the deeper solution: "grace in Christ." Jesus lived in the same world as Teri does, facing the same kinds of people doing the same kinds of things. He sympathizes with her weakness and understands her struggle. He can help her. He was tempted like Teri, and yet remains without sin. He died for the Teri who typically fails when tempted. He is truly tenderhearted towards her, giving mercy and grace that can actually help her. He deals gently with her ignorance and waywardness and teaches her to obey him in new, constructive ways.

Identifying Teri's sufferings, sins, and Savior is not difficult for anyone attuned to biblical categories. (Her mom, boss, friends, and therapists can name her "patterns." But they cannot name them for what they are, or name the Person who is the solution.) In fact, Teri already knows enough of the Bible and herself to know these general truths – sort of. But truth has no traction in her life. It never gets to specifics.

When you know these things, you know the panorama versions of Teri and Scripture. You know the "patterns" inside and out. Perhaps you yourself have done a topical Bible study on "fear of man," or read Edward Welch's book on the subject, *When People Are Big and God Is Small*.[4] Perhaps you've studied Hebrews and seen why Christ gives solid reasons for God's people to embrace the "word of encouragement." Should you have Teri do those studies, read that book, or listen to sermon tapes? At the right time, any of these could be very helpful. But nine times out of ten I'd begin at a different place. I'd want to make some sense of things before she tried to study. And when she does some of those studies, I'd work hard to make sure that she always gets to the place where timely text meets current struggle.

Where did Teri and I begin? We looked at one significant bit of her life and one relevant bit of Bible, talking through both simultaneously. This article can't capture all of our conversations, but I can at least point to where we camped out.

One Bit of Life

We decided to start with Teri's problems in the workplace. She has a coworker who regularly manipulates her into doing extra work, and Teri can't/doesn't/won't say "No." Why did we choose this scene?

First, it's the *simplest* of many similar scenarios with boyfriend, mother, and church. And it comes up almost daily.

Second, the workplace is *significant*. A meaningful skirmish in The Great War can take place in the secretary pool on Friday afternoon. In counseling, I'm always looking for the "laboratory of change." What is the small stage on which big things about God and about Teri are playing out right now?

Third, Teri is *motivated* to start here. It's a constant struggle. She's frustrated with herself. She knows she's being duped, but still can't seem to help it. Troubles with parents and boyfriends have been deeper and more defeating. The struggle at work doesn't seem as overwhelming as those other arenas. To grow here would be a small but significant step in the right direction.

Fourth, the *God-substitute* that routinely hijacks Teri's heart does so in this small setting. When truth retakes the controls here, it will send ripples through her other relationships. To work through how and why she's manipulated at work will help her to wrestle with the sin pattern that plays out everywhere else. The basic insights, truths, skills, strategies, and pitfalls can be generalized to be used elsewhere.

One Bit of Bible

If 100 Christians sought to help Teri handle her workplace more faithfully, they might work from seventy-five different passages and have good reasons in each case. I chose to work with a passage from Hebrews:

> He himself has said, "I will never desert you, nor will I ever forsake you," so that we confidently say, "The LORD is my helper, I will not be afraid. What will man do to me?" (Heb. 13:5b-6)

Why did I choose this particular passage for Teri? Answering this helps us understand why the other seventy-four passages might be equally helpful. It also helps you become more self-conscious about why you choose the passages you do.

First, I've often worked with it. I know it from the inside. I know what it means and how it works. I know how it connects to people and the wider context of God's revelation. I've seen its dynamic work out in different people facing various troubles.

Second, it's short and memorable. The words take Teri by the hand and lead her home. God says and does something wonderful and necessary; she says and does something radical and life-changing.

Third, it's about Teri's problem. These words address people who feel threatened by others. They communicate the courage of faith that is the opposite of fear. Her situation is not exactly the same as the original hearers: financial loss or prison (the first readers of Hebrews); possible death and defeat in war (the people who first heard God make this specific promise in Deuteronomy 31:6); being surrounded by hateful people (the first person to talk to God using these exact words in Psalm 118:6). But the text is intended by God to fit her personalizations. Teri and I use Hebrews 13:5-6 in exactly the same way that the pastor who wrote Hebrews used the two Old Testament bits of Bible to speak to his people's current struggle.

Fourth, this passage contains the three core ingredients of the change dynamic: *orientation, promise, and response*. These words *orient* Teri to the moral landscape of her current struggle. If she chooses fear of man, it leads to cowardice; if she chooses faith, it leads to courage. Teri put it this way: "When I erase God, I become terrified of what people can do to me. When I give in to their excessive demands, I can see that fear of man rules me. I feel alone and overwhelmed. But when I remember this verse, it means that God is with me right now. I'm not alone. If he promises to help me, the whole situation is different, and I'm different, too. It makes perfect sense then to say 'No' firmly but graciously."

The *promise* of God also meets Teri in Hebrews 13:5. God invades her workplace with key aspects of his mercy: "The fact that God himself is talking (*'He himself* has said'), and what he actually says about his love (*'I* am with you; *I* will never leave you.'), speak right into my life when I feel threatened."

Finally, Hebrews 13:6 invites Teri to *turn* and walk out the response: "He leads me out of my typical sins. When I believe the lie, I wimp out. When I believe the truth and trust him, I stand up to people. God demonstrates the response of faith I can make. This is so specific, it's as though he's personally walking me through what faith and courage think like and feel like and act like."

Fifth, I myself have lived this passage, which matters a great deal in ministry. In 1979, I went to Uganda after the overthrow of Idi Amin. Our team worked helping orphans, doing street preaching, and training pastors. Kampala was in anarchy. Gun battles took place every night. Gangs of looters shot it out with each other and with soldiers (who were little more than looters themselves). One evening, we watched an innocent man rushing home five minutes after curfew, stopped by soldiers, pleading for his life, gunned down, his body kicked into a ditch. We had no defense should violent men choose to break in. We were afraid! And the orientation-promise-and-response of Hebrews 13:5-6 wove into my life. God said, "I will never leave you." I learned to say with all my heart, "You are my helper. I will not be afraid. What can man do to me?", and then to walk out the implications. Since then, this dynamic of orientation, gospel, and response has become more and more my own. So when Teri and I talk about Hebrews 13, I communicate first-hand knowledge, not theories attached to Bible verses.

A FINAL WORD

A bit of Teri's life and a bit of God's self-revelation came together in the events she faced that week. We first talked about all this on a Tuesday. Teri didn't dare try anything different on Wednesday or Thursday, but the wheels were turning inside, and friends were praying for her. Friday she took a deep breath, asked God for help, and said to her coworker, "No, I can't do that. I've got other work I need to finish today." The coworker blew up at her. But later that afternoon they had a good talk for about five minutes right before leaving work. On Monday, the coworker was friendlier and even opened up with Teri, confiding some personal problems. A bully-doormat relationship began to change into a give-and-take relationship.

Of course, Teri still had a long way to go. We all do. But she began walking in the right direction. She continued to make significant, courageous choices. She forgave her mother and expressed love to her more forthrightly, mercifully, and generously. She was more resistant and less resentful when her mother tried her familiar manipulations. Teri demonstrated real wisdom in the way she thought through a major family crisis. She helped the family come to a decision, rather than just staying in the background. She became much more constructively involved in her church. She even went back to talk with her former fiancé, and they had an honest personal reconciliation. Her confusion, anxiety, and depression were gradually replaced by an increasing clarity, resolve, purpose, and joy.

You know the problem of the disconnect all too well. May God give you the joys of the reconnect!

7   ILLUSTRATIVE COUNSELING

Good preachers know that when God's truth comes clothed in story and picture, their sermon lives and breathes, and seizes the hearts of hearers. What is true in homiletics also applies to personal, face-to-face ministry. The things that make for a good sermon also make for a good conversation between two people on a Tuesday afternoon. The personal and immediate interchange of conversation is a fertile ground for "illustration."

Biblical counseling, properly understood, intends to serve and enhance prayer and the ministry of the Word in the context of tangible love for people. (See Acts 6:1-5.) The activities we call "preaching and teaching" and those we call "counseling and daily conversation" are two facets of a single activity: the ministry of the Word. Serving others with God's counsel is founded in prayer. It is wrapped in generous actions and attitudes. Biblical counselors must establish an unbreakable connection between the public and private ministries of Christ's grace and truth. They must show practical care for people that provides living illustrations.

Why must we do illustrative counseling? In the first place, conversations are largely composed of stories, of "narrative." Whether the counseling you do is formal or casual, you plunge into a swirl of conflicts, aspirations, joys, and concerns. You will often witness the central themes of a person's life playing out within a single, short anecdote. A prime goal of counseling is to rework the meanings assigned to those stories. You seek to map the story of God's working onto the details of life. Another prime goal of counseling is to influence the next chapter in those stories. You seek to infuse "the willing and the doing of God's good pleasure" into the choices that will be made tonight, tomorrow, and next Saturday.

Second, people's stories and conversations hand you illustrations and metaphors at every turn. Look for pictures, snapshots that capture huge themes. Listen for a word or phrase that carries the freight of the real life drama. Much of what you say in response can be organized around the details of the anecdote or phrase. Biblical truth functions best when it is tailored to the person (counseling, conversation, personal devotions) or to the audience (preaching, teaching, public worship). Timely illustrations are the tailor's scissors and sewing machine. Illustration makes God's truth your truth. Don't dare trample on the Word of God by responding to the vivid stories people tell with only the bare bones of abstract principle and formal doctrine. Ransack the "human documents" for illustrations.

Third, the counseling conversation itself is a further chapter of the same story. The continuing saga unfolds in "real time," here and now. Don't dare trample on the ministry of the Word of God by offering striking illustrations – but staying at arm's length. You must enter the story. Become a player. Your attitudes and actions ought to communicate all that makes wisdom wise. *You* illustrate what you say: Generosity and kindness. Patience in the process. Solicitude for suffering. Approachability, despite any failure, anguish, and confusion. Palpable humility, not superiority. Tender and probing curiosity. Words and attitudes that reflect a deep understanding of people in their life contexts. Constructive candor. Boldness, to believe and speak the truth. Mercy, which invites sinners, and gives them reasons to turn. Mercy, which consoles sufferers, and gives them reasons to continue. Unwavering commitment to glory and holiness. Even-handed, impartial assessments. A love for what is good; a hatred of what is evil. Living, breathing reliance upon Christ's finished grace, present grace, and future grace. Your words ought to communicate the clarity of biblical teaching and principle, the evocative vividness of good metaphor and gripping story – all wrapped with the compelling force of your integrity. The Bible's teachings and principles must be illustrated by your words *and* by your actions.

RUBEN'S PRIZE TOMATOES

Illustrative counseling fishes in the waters of real life. For example, a couple sought counsel because their marriage was disintegrating. Ruben treated his wife with neglect punctuated by harshness. He also happened to raise prize tomatoes, his "pride and joy." You have yourself a metaphor. What would happen if he totally ignored his tomato plants for weeks on end? What if the only time he paid attention to his garden was when he got ticked off about the weeds? What if he took his hoe and hacked indiscriminately at both weeds and stunted plants? Such carelessness and violence would produce few sweet, juicy tomatoes for his eating pleasure. Ruben's garden would be his shame and sorrow. His behavior would figuratively provoke and discourage the plants he ought to nourish and cherish. Marital failure starkly contrasts with gardening expertise. Counseling can highlight that contrast. Gardening illustrates sin or cherishing. Ruben *knows* what you are talking about. He can *remember* it. Huge issues throb with inescapable reality. That's what an illustration does for you.

Neglect and harshness violate the call to nourish and cherish. But Ruben doesn't just need to be convicted and inspired by God's law. He also needs a fresh start. Christ's grace has been nothing more than religious words in a religious book uttered by religious functionaries on religious occasions. Go fishing in the waters of Scripture as well as in Ruben's life. Bible stories and Bible pictures show the love of Jesus for sinning people. They map straight onto this man's life. Many of the pictures happen to be agricultural! "I am the vine, and you are the branches, and my Father is the vinedresser" (John 15). Will Ruben draw life from the main stalk? Will he be lovingly pruned, or cut off and thrown in the compost pile? The truth about Jesus – which has direct implications for Ruben – is like seed scattered on the ground (Luke 8). Will this man prove to be a well-turned, well-watered, and well-weeded garden plot? Or will he prove to be a sidewalk, rock pile, or weed patch?

Ruben has a serious problem. The small-time neglect and harshness he deals out daily are earning him a payback: big-time abandonment and violence. But Jesus took the slashing stroke of the hoe, was forsaken and tortured so that this selfish husband might not have to harvest what he has sown. Jesus' story reworks the elements in Ruben's story. Story rewrites story; picture redraws picture. The ministry of the Word to an individual involves illustrative counseling.

And, of course, the illustrations involved in ministry are not just word pictures and word stories. Your own reactions to Ruben form part of the new story, too: 1 Corinthians 10:12-13 and 1 Thessalonians 5:14. You are meant to *demonstrate* how a good gardener nourishes and cherishes his plants. You are able to identify with Ruben's sins: "No temptation has overtaken you that is not common to all." You are confident of God's aid: "God is faithful." You are bold and direct, kneading the metaphor into the man's life: "Admonish the unruly." You are tender, hanging in and hanging on through the ups and downs of the process: "Encourage the faint-hearted. Hold on to the weak. Be patient with them all." You participate in Ruben's story today, tending the garden, sowing and nurturing tomato seeds, digging up weeds only. Your manner towards his sins illustrates the very ways a husband ought to treat the failings of his wife. Ministry, by illustrative word and illustrative deed, has a ravishing fragrance. Illustrative counseling lifts prisoners out of prison. It strikes sledgehammer blows on the plaster wall of lies. It holds on tight. It persistently speaks reason and hope into the madness of sin.

DAMSEL IN DISTRESS

Here is another picture, another story. Holly is a young woman who shrinks before life's challenges. Suffering and responsibility, however light, terrify her. She fears failure and rejection. She drifts towards laziness. She's a fragile hot-house orchid. Holly tells of how powerful people did – and still do – despise her. She describes herself as "a damsel in distress," swooning into helplessness, waiting for a noble rescuer to ride into her life. Her cravings for comfort, acceptance, adoration, a husband, control, and self-righteous vindication are all captured in that one vivid phrase. Past rejections and present anxieties preoccupy her; she has no goals for the future. Condemning voices can crowd her mind, sabotaging faith and action, guiding her reactions down dead-end streets. But despite the litanies of darkness that often still intone in her head, Holly *has* been significantly changed by Christ. She seeks God; she loves needy people; she loves Christ.

The Bible's pictures inject hope and stability into her stories of crisis and distress. For example, Isaiah 40-66 turns on the lights and turns up the volume, relentlessly placing the Lord himself before Holly's eyes. The Redeemer speaks comfort to sufferer and sinner. He says to his daughter, "*You* are precious in *my* sight, and I love *you*" (43:4-6). The Servant experienced life the way Holly does, and then some. He knows suffering. He bore humiliation and disgrace at the hands of others. He was tried in every way she is. He cried for deliverance and trusted the God who alone vindicates. He did not fear condemnation from any mere man. He listened to the voice of God, not the voices of people. He was a man of action and conviction amidst trial. (These truths thread through Isaiah 50:4-10.)

God presses reality into Holly's unreality. "I made you. I see you. I love you. I pioneered the path you must walk with me. Daughter of the Maker of heaven and earth, listen to the louder, weightier, truer, brighter voice." Holly fears that her afflictions mean abandonment – but Isaiah 49:13-16 portrays a nursing mother's fierce, alert passion. Holly gets snagged by familiar sins, dragged into a tightening spiral of guilt and shame, but Isaiah 52:13-53:12 reveals the innocent, bloodied Lamb triumphantly alive. Holly's parents have mocked her Christian faith as a feeble crutch that can't bear the weight of her problems. She herself is tempted to abandon God, but Isaiah 66:23-24 tells how every knee shall bow and transgressors shall lie down in torment. Holly feels like too much of a failure for God to ever work in her, but Isaiah 61:1-3, 10-11 presents the Rescuer tailored to the afflicted and needy.

In the irony of redemption, as the damsel in distress repents of the need for human rescue as her gravest sin, she finds the Rescuer. Repentant, intelligent faith grows luminous and steady in the Light. Holly finds herself less forlorn, more able to stand, more diligent in tackling life – grace means courage! Holly learns to make different choices because the Person is near. The Word of God floods her with images of the Redeemer. He wows us all and woos us. He badgers us and delights us. He threatens us and comforts us. "If you seek *me* . . . you will find *me*." Isaiah is divine show-and-tell. Look! Listen! Christ imprints who he is and what he does upon lives. His story is rewriting Holly's story. Not once and done, but once and again, and again, and again, until one day the damsel will be no more. The confident daughter and radiant bride will stand. God's metaphors rework our metaphors.

You, too, are an illustration in the unfolding process. You must model the patience, passion, and presence of which you speak. Ministry is intensely personal. You, too, are tender towards sufferer and sinner. Holly ought to feel the imprint of your care: "Like a shepherd he will tend his flock, in his arm he will gather the lambs, and carry them in his bosom; he will gently lead the nursing ewes" (40:11).

Pastoral care is one of God's communicable attributes. You hate the culturally prevalent lies that Holly buys: "They do not know, nor do they understand. . . . A deceived heart has turned him aside" (44:18, 20). Heart-probing discernment is another of God's communicable attributes. You bring good news to Holly as good news, with tears and cheers, thunder and whisper, quiet comfort and firm conviction. She ought to feel the imprint of your faith. For you are alive to the Person you represent and of whom you speak.

Of course, you are not the One who "measured the waters in the hollow of his hand"; nor the One who "as his counselor has informed him" (40:12-13). You are only the servant, reflection, image, counselee and peer counselor. He is the Master, Light, Maker, Wonderful Counselor. If you hear, know, trust, and obey such a God, then Holly will have every opportunity to prosper in your counsel.

Ministry to individuals thrives on story, picture, and incarnation, just like ministry to crowds. Preach the Word – vividly. Counsel the Word – vividly. Clothe the bones of biblical teaching and principle in the flesh of drama, metaphor, and integrity. Tomato growers and distressed damsels play out dramas of cosmic significance in seemingly insignificant incidents. Ministry maps God's truth onto the details of life.

THE PORCUPINE IN THE FOREST

I will close with one final example of illustrative counseling. Jim is thirty-two, married four years, a committed and well-taught Christian. His church just completed a twelve-week series through Ephesians. Jim knows Ephesians 4:17-32: don't live any longer in the ignorant way people instinctively live. He joined his Sunday school class in memorizing Ephesians 4:15 and 4:29: say what helps others to grow. Jim even took careful notes during the sermon on how to treat wives: love, bathe, nourish, cherish. But his wife, Pamela, is seriously malnourished and unloved. He reluctantly came in to counsel at her strong urging. She is frustrated and discouraged by his private, prickly ways. Jim provides well, is committed to her, is not volatile or violent. But he holds her at arm's length, rather than moving towards her. He does not welcome her into his life, or inquire after her welfare. He does not listen to her, seek to understand her, or pray for her. He does not give to her, or forgive her. He does not say constructive and gracious things. He does not consider her interests, but is self-preoccupied. Jim agreed that everything Pamela said was true and commented, "I know, I'm just an old porcupine, and always have been. I know she tries a lot harder than I do, and gives a lot more. I don't really have any major reasons to complain about her."

With that statement, Jim gave us our tailor-made metaphor. An "old porcupine" bears an uncanny resemblance to the "gentiles" of Ephesians 4:17 and the "old man" of 4:22! Such a critter lives in service to deceitful lusts. He violates each aspect of "speaking the truth in love," neither loving, nor speaking truth, nor helping others grow. A disconnect existed between Jim's

Bible knowledge and his life. "Porcupine" helped make the connection. It became a picture – for him, for Pamela, for me – that summarized Jim's instinctive and well-practiced sins. "Porcupine" became our shorthand for where Christ works to rebuild him and give him grace.

Here are some of the details captured by the word picture:

- Jim lived as if the only time to connect with his wife was during mating season, like a solitary porcupine in the woods. Sexual desires alone motivated him to engage his wife. But to become a man, not a brute beast, is to move towards her to build companionship.
- Jim put up his quills at any sense of threat, largely a "defensive" act to keep Pamela at bay. It reflected his fear of being controlled or criticized. Jim's social experience was largely one of fear and self-concealment, arising from cravings for autonomy, self-vindication, and comfort. But to become fully human is to welcome, to listen, to forgive, to pursue, and to love with courage.
- His withdrawal was also a hostile act. He'd get irritated and prickly, leaving Pamela hurt, frustrated, her face full of quills. His pride was expressed in the way he balled up to protect himself and hurt his wife. But to grow in the image of God means to turn from instinctive evils, to do good, to be kind and patient.
- Jim loved to tinker in the backyard on various projects. Often Pamela would pine indoors, handling the parental and household responsibilities, going to bed alone, while Jim did his hobbies until 10:30 or 11:00 at night. He was not a domesticated creature. His evening activities were determined by his personal pleasures. But to become like Jesus is to die to self and follow the Man who laid down his life for his wife.
- Jim's porcupine motif played out in other relationships, too. He was generally antisocial; but Ephesians 4 calls forth God's new society. He interacted minimally with his children; but Ephesians 6 tells fathers to raise their children. His self-reliant quills kept God at bay, too. He was a

functional deist rather than a sheep living under a Shepherd's voice. But relationship with Christ is the beating heart of Ephesians 1-6.

- Jim had in fact "always been this way." But the porcupine – the Bible's comparable animal metaphor is "snake-like" – must come to live as a sheep in God's flock. Having received the intervention of grace, a disciple learns and changes, seeking more grace.

Ephesians tells porcupines to change, and tells how. Christ has good things in mind for Jim. A redemption through blood has been bought, forgiveness for those who look honestly and confess. A surpassingly great power works on the inside to renew. The Lord converts an irritable, fearful, self-willed porcupine into a real man. Jim can be remade into a saint, a warrior, a dwelling place of God in Christ, a partaker in and imitator of the love of God, a beholder of glory, a participant in the community of people growing out of childish ways. He can be remade into a husband.

You as counselor dare not speak bare abstractions to Jim. He'll just nod his head one more time at church talk. You don't dare simply speak vividly illustrated and applied truths. "That was a great sermon, preacher." You must act into his life in the very ways you want him to change. Pursue Jim. Welcome, inquire, listen, pray, forgive, and you will be able to say constructive and gracious things to help Jim grow up.

Tomato farmer meets Vinedresser. Rescuer finds damsel in distress. Porcupine becomes a man. Ruben, Holly, Jim, you. Ministry hands you details, stories, and illustrations in every conversation. The Bible hands you such things, and bids you to work with them. Exegete the person and exegete the Word with equal diligence, so that you might speak and act wisely. Do this. Live this. Pray this. Your counseling will have drama, poetry, music, immediacy, personalness . . . . and impact on lives.

8   TALK INCESSANTLY? LISTEN INTENTLY!

Well might the sun in darkness hide
    and shut his glories in,
When Christ, the mighty Maker, died
    for man the creature's sin.
Thus might I hide my blushing face
    while his dear cross appears;
Dissolve my heart in thankfulness,
    and melt mine eyes in tears.
But drops of grief can ne'er repay
    the debt of love I owe;
Here, Lord, I give myself away,
    'tis all that I can do.

> \- Isaac Watts
> "Alas! and did my Savior bleed"

We live in a day of skeptical, laid-back, carefully measured commitments. We live in a day of half-hearted loyalties, except for those to self-interest, private addiction, self-pity, and a sense of righteous grievance. We live in a day when airing one's opinion matters more than listening intently.

But Christ wants listeners. He wants whole hearts. How does he gain this audience? He tells us to listen and then tells us about *himself*. He communicates this rational, solid, bluntly historical message. This is what Isaac Watts heard. Such hearing elicited intense emotion: profound and appropriate shame, utter gratitude, melting sorrow. Such intent, receptive listening compelled action: "Here, Lord, I give myself away." What so moved him? One supreme truth pierced him heart, soul, mind, and might, and made him respond with self-abandoning love: Christ, the mighty Maker, died for man the creature's sin.

Are you listening?

INCESSANT TALKERS

Recently a friend wrote me, describing the opportunities before her and the strengths and weaknesses she perceived in her counseling:

> Many different people seek me out: sick, bereaved, singles, lonely, stuck, non-Christians, poor, rich, educated, and non-educated. I really love most of them. The ones I have a hard time with talk incessantly . . . . Interpersonal conflict is possibly my forte. I am thrilled when God, through me, brings hope to broken relationships. I may become an expert on anxiety, anger, and fear of man, as these are prominent areas in my life that constantly need pruning. Our heavenly Father does not waste any of it.

Honest words, hammered out of an honest, examined life before God. Her words made me pause. I felt glad that many different people in this bent world were seeking help from someone with wise help to give. I rejoiced that our Father wastes nothing of his freely given – and our hard-won – growth in grace. I know that this woman had also *heard* the things that Isaac Watts heard: the mighty Maker's death for the creature's sin. She, too, rejoiced in the debt of love she had incurred.

I was also struck by the sort of person she found difficult: "The ones I have a hard time with talk incessantly." I could identify. With some people, conversation approximates sitting near a stranger with a boom box. You are compelled to hear, but it's like being forced to overhear someone else's music, being rendered speechless by voluminous speech.

Incessant talkers. Such people not only are a problem, they

have a problem. A pungent Proverb notes, "Where words are many, sin is not absent" (10:19 NIV). Another comments ironically, "Even a fool, when he keeps silent, is considered wise" (18:28). A talker who never stops to listen is in trouble.

GROWING BY LISTENING

The Bible says repeatedly that we grow and change only by listening, not by talking. With good reason Jesus says, "He who has ears to hear, let him hear." With good reason David utters God's call for us to hear pointedly personal counsel: "I will instruct *you* and teach *you* in the way which *you* should go; I will counsel *you* with my eye upon *you*." Failure to listen defines one as a mulish beast (Ps. 32:8-9). Willingness to listen is itself a significant aspect of repentance and renewal.

How might you break in on the overly talkative? The first part of the process looks easy. You have little choice in the matter. You listen. Here's the hard part: you do have a choice about *how* you listen. Listen well. Don't go numb; don't just go along; don't get irritated; don't run for the exit. Listen so you'll understand. Understand so you'll be able to talk with well-aimed words of life, so you'll know how to love. You can't know what to say or do until you have heard the story, the chaotic flood of anecdote, emotion, reaction, interpretation, repetition, contradiction. No surprise, as the proverb alerts us, you will almost invariably hear sins in the process. You'll hear bitterness, gossip, self-pity, false belief, rationalization, obsession, evasion, fabrication – the thousand tongues of foolish and empty talk.

TURNING THE TALKATIVE INTO LISTENERS

Then you must pursue opportunity to speak. Here the battle for souls is joined. What will you say? There's no script, but here's one line of approach I've seen prove fruitful.

- "I've heard you . . . and I've heard you say . . . " Here you can communicate loving concern and understanding.
- "Have I understood you?" Here you can stand corrected. Partial understandings can be supplemented by what you previously did not know.

- "God says we change by listening, not by talking." Let
  God's reality rattle instinctive assumptions. Many incessant talkers have been too busy ever to really think about
  things. They just talk, or talking makes them feel better,
  or they assume that talking will solve things. Inject a different perspective into the verbal stream of consciousness: "Think about this. God says we change by listening,
  not by talking." That's radical! And those who listen
  begin to change the way they talk. They learn to say
  things worth listening to. This is one truth that can be
  documented on every page of Scripture! James 1:18-22 is
  one good place to make a more intentional start.
- "Do you want to hear an honest, constructive response to
  what you've said?" <u>Invite listening</u>. Here hold in mind
  that your call is defined by Ephesians 4:15-16, 25, 29:
  Speak the truth in love . . . do your part . . . speak truth-
  fully . . . speak constructively and graciously. <u>To invite listening is to invite commitment to a genuine interaction
  rather than a perpetual monologue.</u> Some people will say
  no. They prefer to play the same old songs on the boom
  box. But many people will say yes. Christians are, by
  definition, people with "ears to hear." Of course, ears for
  Christ's voice may be momentarily deafened or distracted
  by other voices. <u>But the Shepherd's sheep will hear his
  voice.</u> Bank on it.
- And so you speak timely and appropriate words. There's
  no script, but a conversation that has gotten this far has
  boundless possibilities for fruitfulness.

A SIMPLE MESSAGE

What does an incessant talker need to hear? The same
things as anyone else! A wise pastor, seasoned by decades of
experience with real people's sins and sufferings, once spoke
with me about his approach to counseling. The more he had
come to know himself, other people, and Christ, the more the
basic structure of his counseling had become lean and focused.
He summarized it in a single sentence: "Christ died for all, so

that they who live might no longer live for themselves, but for him who died and rose again on their behalf" (2 Cor. 5:15).

That about says it all. He didn't mean that counseling is simplistic, that people can be crammed into molds. Biblical counsel is supple, infinitely adaptable, able to be personalized to persons and problems. But biblical counsel is also simple. The basic structure and drive of counseling worthy of the name can be stated in one sentence. What does the incessant talker need to stop and hear? Christ died for all, so that they who live might no longer live for themselves, but for him who died and rose again on their behalf.

The hymn by Isaac Watts restates this with suitable emotion and commitment:

> Christ, the mighty Maker, died
> for man the creature's sin . . . .
> Here, Lord, I give myself away.

"The ones I have a hard time with talk incessantly." But the ones who learn to listen find their mouths filled with wonderful grace, freely given. They find Christ himself.

How Do You Help a "Psychologized" Counselee?

I met Sabrina, a thirty-one-year-old single woman, when her mother brought her to counsel with me several years ago. Sabrina had agreed to meet me once, largely to please her mother. After four years in psychotherapy, Sabrina seemed increasingly confused, self-absorbed, friendless, and depressed.

When Sabrina first walked in the room, I noticed John Bradshaw's *Homecoming* wedged in her purse. At that time it was a popular self-help book in which sin and misery (my terms for problems he vividly describes!) are said to arise when "dysfunctional" families fail to meet the love needs of their members. The pure "inner child" within each of us becomes contaminated and wounded and a life of misery, rage, compulsion, and shame results. The "codependent" strives endlessly to fill the empty tank of love, but is always disappointed.

Bradshaw's solution is to find a support group and a therapist that can begin to fill the need and teach techniques of self-affirmation. Bradshaw's testimony to his own "healing" through this gospel threads through the book. He has learned to affirm, express, and indulge himself. He claims to reconnect with his inner I AM-ness, and to find a new life of wonderful, joyful freedom. He urges the reader by exhortation and example to do likewise.

Sabrina's Story

That was John Bradshaw's story, but he was not in the room

with me. Sabrina was. I met the devotee, not the master. So I asked Sabrina to tell me her story. She described herself as a professing Christian who, since her teens, had been earnest in her devotional life and active in her church. Longstanding tendencies to social anxiety, loneliness, and discouragement had worsened about five years earlier, prompting her to seek help from a psychotherapist. Over the previous three years, her relationship to God had "gone stale, and God seemed far away." A note of peevishness and self-pity crept into the way she talked about God. All those truths that Christian doctrine proclaimed seemed barren compared to the deep things she kept discovering about herself through her therapy and reading. God was a disappointing person. Unsurprisingly, habits of Bible reading, prayer, public worship, and ministry had slackened. Even when she was "faithful," she was going through the motions.

The grievous effects of living in a fallen world had not left Sabrina untouched. Her father had betrayed the family, leaving when she was fourteen years old. Her mother, cowed by years of his angry outbursts and adulteries, had been largely ineffectual. Sabrina's peer culture was obsessed with beauty, popularity, possessions, and athletic success. Sabrina had bought the value system, and largely failed against it. The breakup of the family and her obsession with largely unobtainable goals bred turbulent emotions and behavior. After several years of promiscuity (one way to obtain at least the illusion of desirability) Sabrina found Christ when she was seventeen. She had joyously embraced forgiveness and a new life, and lived a life of sexual purity thereafter. But the patterns of her heart that had once driven her immorality did not yield so rapidly. Many things in her life had stabilized. She had gone to college and become a competent elementary school teacher. But as her singleness continued through her twenties, Sabrina's emotions again became more troubling.

She looked for help. Friends recommended a psychotherapist who was a Christian. He had suggested she read *Homecoming*, as well as similar books by both Christians and non-Christians: *Codependent No More* by Melanie Beattie, *Love Is a Choice* by Robert Hemfelt, Frank Minirth, and Paul Meier.

Sabrina had found these books "incredibly meaningful, I saw myself on every page." She was now reading Bradshaw for the fourth time. Her therapist largely adopted the codependency and dysfunctional family theory, Christianizing it by suggesting Sabrina look to Jesus to meet her need for love, because Jesus accepted and affirmed her unconditionally.

Her therapy and reading had aroused a great deal of emotion and had given Sabrina the sense that she was continually discovering profound things about herself. But she still lived in a gray world, and for all the self-discovery, her life was unraveling. Neither Bradshaw nor therapy nor Jesus seemed able to give her hope, vitality, or significant change.

Sabrina is a classic "psychologized" person. She has been discipled into a way of processing her problems that effectively excludes what is most deeply true about God, herself, and her world. And her misunderstanding of the Christian life hinders her from probing and processing her problems biblically.

How Do You Help Sabrina?

How do you help Sabrina and others who are convinced that their core problem lies in what somebody else did to them? Or in their opinion of themselves? Or in how they are genetically hardwired or hormonally imbalanced? You likely know people who have been sent on a long wild goose chase, grasping answers that never deliver what they promise. How can you help Sabrina to know the "solid joys and lasting treasures that none but Zion's children know"? Let me suggest a half-dozen things to anchor your work with psychologized people.

Don't underestimate how strongly people hold their beliefs, however confused, and remember that their reasons seem plausible to them. You must dig out those reasons. You must be able to reveal their pretense, next to the beauty and comprehensiveness of the truth. The Bible will always make better sense of the experiences, behaviors, thoughts, emotions, and attitudes that secular psychologies pretend to explain. The psychological explanations Sabrina currently embraces do a number of things for her. They "ring her bells" by accurately describing how some people feel, think, act, and experience. That's the bait. The hook is the false explanation. Popular hooks often restate those symptoms using some bit of technical jargon that gives the illusion of deep explanatory power. "Low self-esteem," "ADD," "codependency," and "dysfunctional family" are examples of such jargon. These terms actually do nothing more than summarize certain troublesome symptoms, but they pretend to describe underlying, "real" causes of problems.[1] They are descriptions masquerading as explanations. Such labels carry an explanatory model that deviates from reality. Both the explanations and solutions invariably lead people away from a biblical understanding of God, sin, suffering, grace, and obedience.

Sabrina needs to be persuaded. You will want to "ring her bells," too. You will want to use true labels that explain life from God's point of view, rather than by evading God. You will want to show her how biblical truth makes sense of her life and leads her out of her problems. How will you accomplish this?

Remember that you are counseling a person, not a book. Sabrina is a wandering sheep, not a false prophet; she is a struggler, not a theory. Sabrina wanted help four years ago, and she took what was out there. What she took is poisonous, pitiful, shallow, and deceptive. I hate what Bradshaw teaches (and one of my goals is to help Sabrina learn to hate it intelligently), but I dare not hate Sabrina. I feel for her in her confusion. And I have no reason, initially, to go after Bradshaw with her. He's not in the room, she is. I want to win her to something better. She doesn't need arguments. Amid her fourth reading of his "incredibly meaningful" book, you'll only discredit yourself if you start attacking it. She first needs something to make better sense of her world than Bradshaw does. What will you give her?

Don't give her what she has already tried and found lacking. The outward forms of Christian devotion have become empty husks for Sabrina, so don't give them right back to her. Find out why they've become empty. You want to feed her the sweet honey of wisdom, the bread of life. But she's been distracted. It will take work, exploration, knowledge – not pat answers – to find and restore the wandering, misled sheep. Assuming that you haven't underestimated her problem, haven't gotten into a needless argument, and haven't given her empty forms, what will you now do?

Care for Sabrina in a way that communicates. Several observations indicate that Sabrina is likely driven by a desire to be loved: (1) Rejection often reveals and intensifies such cravings; (2) Promiscuity expresses their degrading power; (3) The characteristic temptations of singles in their late twenties make it even more plausible; (4) Bradshaw's model easily seduces such people. You want to help set Sabrina free of her beguiling "need" for love. But, paradoxically, you begin by loving her. You bless her with kindness and concern. Though she craves to be "accepted just as I am," accept her God's way – "just as I am, despite who I am, intending to change who I am."

God's grace in Christ and God's agenda for change make Christian love far more powerful and radical than the cheap acceptance she longs for. Let her experience this genuine, Christian kindness. Listen to her story. Take her seriously. Pursue knowing her and her world. Sympathize with her struggles. We serve a Savior who was touched with our infirmities, who then calls us to seek mercy so that we are not deceived and destroyed by sin. We serve a Savior who freely gave bread to hungry people, and then taught bread-idolaters about the Bread of Life. As you care about her, what will you do?

Get to know Sabrina and her world. Wise counsel thrives on details. You can't help someone when you are ignorant. So dig in. You already know she has misinterpreted her real problems – she's "psychologized" – but what *are* her real problems? Expect to find out things about her that, understood biblically, will let you engage her creatively and personally. Expect that when the Word lights up her life, you'll be able to offer her things that she never knew, or has forgotten. Get to know how she thinks, feels, acts, talks, interprets, evaluates. Get to know what has happened to her, what is happening to her, and what she imagines will happen. God is at work in *this* young woman. She is not a generic category, the "psychologized counselee"; she is a specific person to know. Once you know her, where will you start to intervene?

Don't make Sabrina leap tall buildings with a single bound. God puts a stairway – even a handicapped ramp – in front of each one of us. Look for the next step, organic to who Sabrina is. Don't force her into some predetermined mold. God meets people amid their experience. He has designed his universe so that all experience – rightly interpreted – cries out in testimony to the God of Scripture. And every moment presents significant choices. I've known counselors who routinely started with Sabrinas by making them leap a tall building. They would say, "This counseling will be based on the Bible, and your commitment to Christ's lordship must come first." That's entirely the right core commitment for the *counselor* and the right goal for counseling. But it's entirely misguided as a starting point for *this* counselee. All the facts cry out for a different starting point. Explicit discussion of the authority of Scripture and Christ might come five steps down the road, or it might simply get established as a byproduct of the effective ministry of the Word. But it is a "tall building" at this moment. You need to find the next step in the right direction.

The Bible itself begins in many different places. Scripture continually models how God's servants hook the immediate experience and concerns of their hearers. Because they aim to be *heard* by real people in real situations, they don't prepackage their message.

When Paul spoke in Antioch to a Bible-honoring synagogue audience, he could begin by unpacking chapter and verse (Acts 13:14-41). These hearers were ready to grapple with the claims of Christ and the Word. But when Paul spoke to peasants in Lystra, he began by exposing the emptiness of their particular false beliefs, and then moved on to their immediate experience of God's goodness in weather and crops (Acts 14:14-17). It was the appropriate point of contact. And when Paul addressed the intelligentsia in Athens, he engaged their religious practices and literature (Acts 17:16-34).

The core message remained the same in each case: the living God – who reveals himself in the Scriptures and in his creation – calls people to turn from sin to Christ. But Paul could get to the same destination by many routes. Paul was only doing what the prophets and the Lord Jesus had done before him, and what we ought to do after him.

Sabrina gives ample evidence that the authority of Scripture and the lordship of Christ are poor starting points for her. Notice some important things about Sabrina, things we know even based on minimal information. She currently finds the Bible *insignificant* in comparison to her experiences of self-exploration; she finds Christian truths *meaningless* in comparison to John Bradshaw's interpretation of her experience; she finds the orthodox gospel *irrelevant* in comparison to the gospel of a need-meeting Jesus. The fact that neither Bradshaw nor the therapeutic Jesus work makes little difference to her. She is currently fascinated by what you know to be emptiness, and bored by what you know to be fullness.

At the same time, God in his immediate redemptive working has brought Sabrina to you. One of the *goals* of your counseling is to bring her to understand the relevance of the Word of Christ. She doesn't see the relevance; she sees a husk. If you make her commitment to a husk your first step, you fail. You fail Christ, because he meets people on many different footings, and you've failed to find the right point of contact. You fail Sabrina by blundering, and may well repel her from the very truths she most needs.

What might be an appropriate starting point with Sabrina? Her current experience and interpretation of life. You've already started there by avoiding many pitfalls. You've cared for her: that creates a context for trust. You've sought to know her: that gives you the goods to interact intelligently. As you start to speak into her life, you want to make better sense of her life experience than the other voices she's been listening to.

Reinterpret her experience and world biblically. Truth is far better than the deceitful half-truths and fabrications she has embraced. So let God's truth make sense of her life. You haven't viewed her as the enemy; you haven't given her pat answers; you've cared about her; you've gotten to know her; you've looked for the point of contact. Timely and appropriate truth will now shed light into dark places.

1. You want to ring her bells about what happened to her, but to give it a different meaning. She has been taught to view her "dysfunctional family" upbringing as determinative. Help her to see that her family's sins created pressures of temptation, teaching her lies, sinning against her in specific ways. Woe to those through whom stumbling blocks come! God is merciful to sufferers, the refuge of the poor and needy. We dare not return evil for evil. Temptation does not determine our response.

2. You want to ring her bells about how she reacts, but to give it a different meaning. Sabrina has come to view her "codependent lifestyle" as a form of personal dysfunction, not a pattern of sin. Help her to see how her anger, manipulation, abuse of food, social anxieties, and the rest are works of the flesh that arise from her heart.

3. You want to ring her bells about what controls her, but to give it a different meaning. She believes that the deepest problem of her heart is an unmet need for love and acceptance. Help her to see that her heart is ruled by an enslaving demand for such things. It makes perfect sense that God seems far away and biblical truth abstract: she's been worshiping at the altar of another god, and making Jesus the errand boy of that other god's demands. But Jesus never cooperates with deceit in the lives of those he loves. God will never allow one of his choice daughters to be happy serving her idol.

4. She has come to view Jesus as the psychotherapist in the sky, who exists to meet her felt needs. You may not even need to mention this. If you've done your job on the previous three points, you will now be able to help her to see instead the crucified Savior who died for her lusts and lies and the bad fruits that accompany them. He will forgive her, as she sees her real need and seeks him. Help her to seek the Lord whose strength is sufficient to change her. He will help her. She can become free of what traps her and makes her miserable. Christ will help her to be ruled by him and not by her slave-masters.

Help her to take refuge in the One who delivers the oppressed; she can trust rather than fear in the face of hardships.

5. Sabrina is living as if faith were bare assent to doctrines, and obedience were the fulfillment of religious responsibilities. Help her to see that God has much better things in mind for her. He claims her trust, her love, and her dependence. He calls for her obedience, so that she would learn to love others intelligently rather than demand their affirmation and adoration. Bible, prayer, church, and ministry had become husks; they can again express living communication and significant love.

The key to helping psychologized people is to bring truth to bear in a way that explains and addresses their real life problems. If you can't make sense of the details of Sabrina's life, your words will have the same taste as those empty husks. If you make sense, your counsel will drip milk and honey.

Loving the Light

I've spoken with many psychologized Sabrinas. I have found that more often than not they rejoice to embrace biblical truth when it is expressed personally, caringly, and pointedly. They are Christians, after all. They love the light. They love grace. But they've been offered pat answers or psychobabble to solve their real life problems. When the former didn't work, the latter looked attractive and sounded persuasive. Heresies are the unpaid debts of the church, after all. We can be up in arms about Bradshaw and his kind, but we ought to put the great bulk of our energy into doing a better job of making sense of Sabrina. If we pay our debts by deepening our counseling, we will do a far better job than any of the psychologies.

Confusion and despair visibly lifted from Sabrina's countenance over the course of those first couple of hours we spoke. The Bible makes sense of life, and that sense is deeply satisfying. "If you get one thing, get wisdom. Nothing you desire can compare with her." Wisdom is much better than endless, futile efforts to fill a leaking love tank or to prop up a sagging self-esteem. Wisdom is love. Wisdom is joy. Wisdom is peace.

Sabrina had agreed to meet me once. Four years of

psychotherapy and Bradshaw in the purse weigh a lot. But she came back the next week without *Homecoming* in her purse. Her countenance was half clouded over again, but her first words filled me with joy: "You know the things we talked about last week? Could we have that same conversation over again?" We did – or at least an approximation thereof. She again became radiant with hope. She started drawing fresh, rapid-fire connections herself.

The next time we met – perhaps a month later – Sabrina mentioned that she had quit meeting with her therapist. It had seemed thin and empty – a husk. The Word of the living God, prayer to that God, honest and constructive Christian friends, doctrines of grace and truth, ministry to others, these dry bones were already coming back to life. The real issues in her life kept getting addressed, both outside and inside counseling. She saw numerous ways that her craving for human approval and her terror of rejection played out in her life. And she began to find Christ and the courage to love people in those numerous situations. She began to deal with bitterness at her father and disappointment with her mother, forgiving them. She began to try on new ways of relating to them. Her newfound courage was quite remarkable. She started to deal with her own patterns of fear and ineffectualness, and made several major life decisions over the next several months. Sabrina had taken the next step in learning to live life in God's world from the standpoint of faith, rather than in the quicksand of human approval.

Sabrina and I never actually had to deal with Bradshaw head on. Of course, it would be appropriate with some people to take on Bradshaw at the right time. The question is, Where is the point of contact, the next step, with *this* person? When Sabrina started tasting the truth, the counterfeit lost its savor. A couple months later, she commented, "You know, I really have no desire to read those books anymore. It's funny how much I used to think was in them. I thought *I* was in them. But I'm not anymore." Case closed. This psychologized young woman had instead found herself in the Word of the living God.

Part II We Grow Up Together

No one with any instinct for counseling others in the grace and truth of Christ can long duck the question of "the church." The Lord's people are called to help each other grow up. We are called to know and be known by each other. We are called to counsel each other, to be change agents in each other's lives. We are called to speak the truth in love, and make a difference as brothers and sisters, shepherds and sheep. There is a serious misfit between that vision and a system of autonomous mental health professionals treating their clients/patients.

But for many of us, life experience with "my church" and "churches" rarely aligns with the description of the church in Ephesians 4. The very idea of significant, life-rearranging mutual counseling (the central thought of Ephesians 4) often seems alien. For many people, to hear that *the church has primary counseling responsibilities* makes about as much sense as hearing, "The church has primary neurosurgery and post-op responsibilities," or "The church has primary heating, cooling, and plumbing responsibilities."

Huh?! Churches do... well, churchy-type things – you know, worship services, Sunday school, meals to the sick, an annual picnic, the deacons' small scale gifts to get folks through a rough patch, and pastoral visits to pray for hospital patients (though it's really the medicine that makes them better). But counseling?! At best, larger churches might hire a "professional" with essentially secular training. But Christian faith appears to have no intrinsic depth of counseling insight and no essential call to counseling effectiveness.

THE CHURCH'S COUNSELING CALL

To all that, we *ought* to say, "Huh?! What Bible have you not been reading?" "Wake up, O sleeper, rise from the dead, and Christ will give you light!" (Eph. 5:14). Christian faith has intrinsic depth and an essential call to counseling wisdom, whether or not we've gotten the message yet.

Our experience of church – locally, nationally, or globally – might appear worlds apart from "the church" as the Bible describes it. But what else is new? Our individual lives appear worlds apart from Jesus' life. To pick one example, Jesus is a wonderful counselor. He cuts to the heart. He's inconceivably generous and merciful. He's eminently approachable. He asks great questions. He's fiercely tough-minded. And he turns lives upside down. In comparison, we might be bumbling, mis-guided, ignorant, ineffectual, harsh, or timid. We might not even want to think of ourselves as counselors – though from Jesus' point of view, all of us are always counselors, whether foolish or wise. Sure, we've got a long way to go. But it is into that image of Jesus that we are all being transformed. It is our joy that such a transformation turns churches into communities of wise love.

Part II of this book focuses on churches as the location of choice for wise counseling ministry. These nine chapters seek to rearrange how we think about "church," about "counseling," and about "ministry." They move from the big picture towards a selection of practical implications. As in Part I, I offer core samples, not a complete excavation of the topic of counseling in the church. But I hope you will catch a vision that will ani-mate you to press in *this* direction with all your might for as long as it takes.

Chapter 10, "What Is 'Ministry of the Word'?," seeks to rat-tle long-held assumptions about ministry. One big reason we don't grasp the counseling call of the church is that we wear blinders when it comes to Word ministry. We rightly see that public ministry from the pulpit is crucial, but we often fail to see that interpersonal ministry in conversations is equally so. In fact, the quality of conversations in the church is proof of whether public ministry is succeeding or failing to achieve Christ's goals.

"Counseling *Is* the Church" (Chapter 11) seeks to rattle habitual assumptions about "church." When the Bible describes the church in action, it describes a community in which timely, pointed, personal counseling is continually taking place. Many commitments, skills, and institutional innovations are needed to bring such communities into existence.

Chapter 12 takes the vision presented in these chapters and focuses on one practical implication. Where can you start to build and strengthen the mutual counseling within any group of Christians? "What Will You Ask For?" examines the fresh opportunities that lie within something Christian people already do. We make prayer requests of each other, and we pray to God. Think more carefully about what you want. Re-jig what you ask for to align better with what God says we need. You will open the door to better mutual counsel.

The next two chapters approach counseling in the church from two different but complementary directions. Chapter 13, "Pastoral Counseling" looks at the counseling ministries of pastors. Within the varied responsibilities a pastor has for preaching and congregational leadership, what percentage of time should he give to conversational ministry?

Chapter 14, "Counseling Under the Influence of the X Chromosome" looks at counseling done by women in the church. It considers to how women tend to think about people and counseling. The implications of what women say and do to help others will help all believers, male or female, pastor or layperson, to counsel more wisely.

As the church assumes the tasks and responsibilities of counseling, it naturally brings into sharp focus the question, "Do You Ever Refer?" to psychologists or psychiatrists (Chapter 15). "Of course" is the naïve answer. "Never" is the narrow-minded answer. As we learn to ask the right questions, we can answer this question more carefully.

The final two chapters in Part II consider how to implement two matters of concern for all God's people. Chapter 16, "Why I Chose Seminary for Counseling Training," looks at counselor training. When we understand what counseling *must* be about, we see the logic of distinctively Christian training.

Chapter 17, "Affirmations & Denials" proposes a formal statement of faith to guide the church's endeavors in counseling. Such a statement of faith lacks the pizzazz of the topical essays in the same way that the fence around your garden lacks the pizzazz of the roses or tomatoes growing within. But you need a good fence to shelter and nurture growing things.

10   WHAT IS "MINISTRY OF THE WORD"?

Free-associate with me for a minute. What pops into your head when you hear the phrase "ministry of the Word"? What do you think of when you hear the phrase "proclamation of the gospel"?

Jot down two or three words, phrases, or images that come to mind. You might want to ask friends, members in your church, people you counsel, or coworkers what their associations are as well.

I suspect that at or near the head of most lists you will find such things as "preaching," "pastor giving a sermon," "church on Sunday morning," "street-corner evangelist," "teaching," "pulpit ministry," and "quoting Scripture."

What do all these have in common? Each of them envisions one-way communication. A speaker delivers a prepared message to listeners.

These "preaching" words are certainly legitimate associations. It is certainly good that we associate sermons with Word and gospel! *Public* ministry of the Word of grace and truth is fundamental to the life of the church.

But I hope to reroute your train of associations somewhat.

Imagine if we asked a group of people, "Free-associate to the word *rainbow*," and every person came up with "red, orange, and yellow." Important things are obviously missing, like green, blue, and violet! Similarly, if in our thought experiment, we mainly mention preaching-oriented words, we also miss something very important. In the Bible itself, "ministry of the

Word" and "proclamation of the gospel" are not exclusively (or even primarily) portrayed as what we think of as a sermon from the pulpit on Sunday morning. *Sometimes* the Bible portrays Word and gospel coming via one-way communication. But often it portrays two-way conversations. Grace and truth are ministered in the spontaneous give-and-take of talking, doing, and relating with one another.

INTERPERSONAL MINISTRY OF THE WORD

Perhaps you've heard it said, "If people would only sit under good preaching and have regular personal devotions, they wouldn't need counseling." That statement is well-intended. It's even partly true since lots of personal problems are transformed by *public* ministry of the Word and by *private* ministry of the Word. But the statement is completely untrue in its premises and conclusions. A central purpose of good preaching and private devotions is to create wise counselors and promote mutual counsel! When any personal problem is in fact truly transformed, a wise counselor of others has been produced. Fruitful *interpersonal* ministry of the Word is the main proof that sermons and devotions are worth the time and effort. How do we know this? Let's consider two things.

Wisdom Is a Verbal Virtue

First, wisdom is a highly verbal virtue. It's a conversational skill. Have you ever talked candidly with a truly wise person – someone who is insightful . . . caring . . . honest . . . generous . . . concerned . . . persistent . . . patient . . . curious . . . attentive . . . direct . . . practical . . . humble . . . knowledgeable . . . feeling . . . thoughtful . . . open . . . serious . . . humorous . . . clear . . . and fresh . . . and who lives with Christ Jesus in view at all times? Such wise friends are among life's finest pleasures. Friends that are even a *little* bit like this *some* of the time are fine pleasures! How we long to be like this ourselves, even a little bit, some of the time!

These are communicable attributes of Jesus, who comes full of grace and truth. Do you give and receive such interpersonal ministry of wise love? It's no wonder Proverbs says, "If you get one thing, get wisdom. Nothing you desire can compare with her. She is a tree of life, a garland of grace, exquisite riches, a feast beyond imagination!" (See Proverbs 3 and 8.)

Wisdom is a verbal virtue. Proverbs comes to us in the form of a personal conversation, not as a sermon or a book. The wise father and mother come as counselors: "My son . . . ." The joyously purposeful "Wisdom" is preeminently a counselor. Wisdom is conversational skill. Consider the fact that the most frequent topic of Proverbs is how we talk. What reveals whether or not you fear and trust the Lord God with all your heart? By all means, take a look at your approach to money, sex, work, family, food and drink. Proverbs covers them all. But most often, you just look to the way you *talk* and the way you *listen*.

Christ's Conversational Ministry

A second way that the interpersonal ministry of the Word is affirmed is through Jesus' own ministry of the Word and his own proclamation of the gospel. He often spoke to crowds outdoors and to congregations in synagogues. He gave sermons. But he also did a lot of talking with people – intentional, honest conversation. He counseled the Word. He conversed the gospel. Jesus dealt with the immediate questions and struggles that individuals put to him. He asked questions of them in turn. He talked the same kinds of issues that he preached.

Several years ago I was reading the Gospel of Mark while thinking about these matters. I took apart five chapters (Mark 7-11), looking not for the content of Jesus' teaching, but for its context. I asked, "Is what happens in this scene one-way preaching or two-way conversation?" These observations are not normative in any way. ("You must have the same ratio of interpersonal ministry to public ministry as Jesus has." "You should quote Scripture as often – or as infrequently – as Jesus.") We are only watching and describing.

These five chapters contain twenty-six scenes. Jesus talks in every one, but four scenes are predominantly action. Here Jesus lives his message. He ministers the Word and proclaims the gospel by incarnating the message, arousing faith by actions.

The verbal exchanges are related to his actions. The other twenty-two scenes contain verbal ministry of the Word. How many portray public proclamation to a crowd and how many capture the back-and-forth of interpersonal conversation?

There are four instances of *public ministry*, of sermons to crowds. Only one (8:34-9:1) did not arise from an earlier conversation or lead to a subsequent one.

That leaves eighteen scenes in which Jesus does *interpersonal ministry of the Word*. Jesus converses the Word. He *interacts* the gospel. Is that part of your associations to "ministry of the Word"? No surprise, whether Jesus is preaching or counseling, he puts things in a way that reaches people's hearts. He engages their questions, reactions, thoughts, experiences, troubles, motives, blind spots, circumstances, and hopes.

Jesus counsels. He does depth counseling, pursuing fundamental rearrangements of your *modus operandi*. How? He loves you. He knows you, inside and out. He enters into whatever you face and whoever you are, "For we do not have a high priest who cannot sympathize with our weaknesses, but One who has been tempted in all things as we are, yet without sin" (Heb. 4:15). He carries on honest, wise conversations (and gives wise sermons). He deals with the deepest issues. What do you live for? Where do you try to find identity? How do you interpret what happens to you? How do you treat other people? What do you do with Jesus himself? What goes on with your anger, anxiety, indifference, and passion? Where do you turn when life is hard? What do you want? Fear? Trust? Love? How do changing what you live for and changing how you live go hand in hand?

When you are counseled this way, you learn to counsel this way.

THE WORD IN CONVERSATIONAL MINISTRY

Sometimes in conversation, Jesus cited author, book, and text from earlier Scripture (see Mark 7:6-7, 10; 10:4, 6-9, 19; 11:17). Sometimes he wove the words of earlier Scripture into the conversation without noting the source (8:18; 9:48). But his words were always biblical in their essence. God's intentions and point of view shaped everything he said. Just like a good preacher, counselor, and friend, what Jesus said was always fresh. The same truth always came out differently, because people always differ. Neither a sermon nor a counseling conversation is a collection of Bible quotes. We might even say that Jesus put truth in his own words because he was *ministering* the Word to the specific needs of specific people. (Of course, *his* own words are the Word in a way our own words aren't, but there is still an analogy.)

It shouldn't be necessary to say this, but the most common misunderstanding of "biblical counseling" is the notion that quoting Bible verses is the defining methodological feature. Of course, bringing God's words to lives is central. But if quoting were the defining feature, how could you ever counsel a non-Christian? Yet Jesus counseled non-believers frequently and found it easy to converse about what matters. He was able to love them, to climb into their lives, to go after what ruled their hearts, to give them himself in a fresh and personal way, so that they might come to believe and find mercy, hope, and direction.

For that matter, if Bible citation were the chief methodological distinctive, how could you have a conversation with *anyone*?! Honest and wise conversations (like wise sermons) abound with many things: questions, comments, stories, metaphors, current events, personal details, opinions, asides that double back later, wit, emotion, silences, particularizing emphases, heartfelt concerns – *and* the Word of life, shaping it all. This is how Jesus converses (and preaches).

GOD'S PURPOSES SHAPE OUR CHOICES

The distinctive of biblical counseling is that it is shaped by the worldview and purposes of the Savior God who has given his Word – not that every sentence must contain the word "God" or refer to a text. Whether or not to quote chapter and verse is a choice shaped by wise love for the particular person with whom you are speaking. If you see with biblical eyes and intend with biblical intentions, you are always reaching after the things that matter most. Whom are you living for and how are you living? The "narrow" way of the Messiah bursts with life and truth; the thousand "broad" ways are barren, strewn with disappointed hopes, with miscarriages of what humanness is meant to be.

Ministry of the Word and gospel proclamation: if it happens in public and in private, it should happen interpersonally.

What do you now associate with the phrases in our thought experiment? I hope you will always associate preaching. It was Jesus' "custom," his habit (Mark 10:1), to preach. The Holy Spirit powerfully uses one-way communication to change hearers' lives one by one. But I hope you also form a rich set of associations to two-way communication. The public and private ministries of preaching and devotional study are but two legs of a three-legged stool. Interpersonal ministry of the Word is the third leg. It's the proof of whether or not the furniture can bear the weight.

11 | COUNSELING *IS* THE CHURCH[1]

The things that make the Wonderful Counselor so wonderful include his incommunicable attributes: omniscience and omnipotence. Those abilities that belong to God alone are his to use in every counseling situation. But Jesus generously empowers his disciples with communicable attributes that give us what it takes to counsel well. He teaches us to treat people with wise love that can search out every wrinkle of the human condition. The Redeemer makes under-redeemers who can aid others where they need it. He offers insights, love, and skills that can take root in our lives individually and communally. Wise love, intelligent joy, savvy peacemaking, patient engagement with people over the long haul are what the church is by definition. Counseling is a prime expression of such things. It is what the church (the Wonderful Counselor's trainees) is *about*.

That assertion raises a thousand questions. In this chapter I'm going to focus not on our "faith and practice" (Christ's vision for "theory and therapy"), but on our institutional structures, Jesus' take on the system we seek to establish. Does that sound boring? It's not. We're social beings by creation, not hedgehogs who burrow alone. Social creatures form communities that are organized in some way, and counseling calls forth many organizational needs. This chapter will turn on two sets of questions regarding our institutions.

WHAT SHOULD BE AND WHAT IS

The first set of questions asks, "What *ought* to be the social structure of counseling if we are to please the Shepherd of the sheep?" What institutional structures ought to be in place for face-to-face ministry? How should care be delivered? What credentials and characteristics define leadership and valid professionalism in the curing of souls? What is the role of one-anothering, friendship, and mentoring? How should the faith and practice (concepts and methods) of our counseling be enriched and regulated to ensure continued faithfulness to God?

The second set of questions asks, "How *is* the church doing?" Are current institutional arrangements viable and valid? Are we meeting the needs? Do we even know what we need? What are the implications for the church of Christ, given the lack of many institutional components necessary for the curing of souls?

The Bible addresses not only ideas and practices, but social structure: institutions, communities, and programs. Does the Holy Spirit intend us to develop the social organization for curing souls? Yes. The church – as the Bible defines it – contains an exquisite blending of leadership and mutuality, of specialized roles and general calling, of truth and love, of wisdom for living, and of flexibility to meet the problems that sinners and sufferers face. The people of God, *functioning* as the people of God, provide the ideal and desirable institution to fix what ails us. That institution can adapt to take on a thousand different problems.

Soul care and soul cure – sustaining sufferers and transforming sinners – is a vital part of the ministry of the church according to the Bible, however poorly we may be doing the job. The Lord whose will the Bible reveals lays claim to the curing of souls. If counseling is about understanding and resolving the human condition, if it deals with the problems of real people, if it ever mentions the name Jesus Christ (or ought to, but doesn't), then it travels in the domain of theology and the curing of souls. "Counseling" ought to come under, and express, the church's authority and orthodoxy.

I include under "church" not only local churches, but also, as qualified below, "meta-church" organizations (associations, denominations, synods, and the like), and Christian workers in "para-church" specialized ministries. Meta- and para-church organizations can often serve useful auxiliary roles with a specialized purpose different from what any particular local church is able to do. Among the valid roles for cooperative ministries, in my view, are education, publishing, and cooperative ministry to meet various needs in a region, hospitals, and missions.

Extramural Christian works need to remember that they are "barely legitimate" in the sense that they ought to exist only when they genuinely and intentionally serve the interests of the communities whose mature functioning will put them out of business. For example, para-church ministry becomes illegitimate when it competes with or uses local churches to its own ends. But that said, there is room for much institutional innovation and development, both within local churches and in meta- or para-church forms. Explicitly biblical truth and love must be tailored to meet particular needs for redemptive help. Among the sorts of special ministries currently valid are crisis pregnancy, counseling, marriage enrichment, prison, and campus programs, as well as ministries to the homeless, the addicted, the elderly, and to immigrants. And there is no reason that both everyday struggles (anxiety, depression, relational conflicts) and "mental health" problems shouldn't also be addressed by specialized, skillful biblical ministries.

What is the state of the church itself regarding the curing of souls? It is not enough for those who believe in this vision to proclaim "The church, the church, the church." The church does not currently have in place many of the necessary commitment statements, educational resources, training arrangements, oversight mechanisms, and practice venues to deliver the goods. Functional autonomy and the potential for confusion and error are not only problems of mental health professionalism. They exist within the church as well.

AN INSTITUTIONAL EXAMPLE

Let me give a concrete example. I am part of the Presbyterian Church in America (PCA). One of the leaders in our congregation, AJ, is pursuing ordination. To be ordained in the PCA, AJ will be tested in many significant areas. His character must match the requirements for Christian maturity and fidelity to Christ. He must be examined in Bible knowledge, theology proper (view of God), soteriology (view of salvation), exegesis (his ability to get at what the Bible says), church history (how we got where we are), church government (how the machinery works), and preaching (his ability to talk to a crowd and communicate true and gracious orthodoxy).

But what about the curing of souls and counseling? AJ will not be examined on what he believes and how he practices ministry to individuals. He will present no case study of a disintegrating marriage or of a woman who binges and purges. There is no tradition of wisdom for the curing of souls into which AJ has been intentionally and systematically discipled. There is no institutional system – creedal, educational, qualifying, or supervisory – to help him think as biblically about counseling as he does about preaching or evangelism. Counseling is a wild card. AJ can believe and do whatever he wants about counseling as long as he can give the right answer to the technical theological questions about sanctification.

Imagine, then, that AJ must deal with Roger, a troubled church member. Roger is given to fits of rage, bouts of depression, and restless anxiety. His relationships with others are poor, and his work history is spotty. As a pastor in the PCA, AJ could take many different approaches towards this member of Christ's flock. Roger could be sent to a secular psychiatrist for Prozac to level his moods. He could be sent to a Meier New Life Clinic and be taught the principles of *Love Is a Choice*. Perhaps AJ himself could counsel Roger, exploring his pain and disappointment at his parents, to refocus his longings for relationship onto the Lord. Or AJ might treat Roger as frustrated in his search for significance, needing Jesus to help him feel good about himself.

AJ could attempt to identify and cast out demons of anger that became attached to Roger's family line through the sins of previous generations and which now hold him in bondage. Roger could be referred to a secular psychologist for cognitive-behavioral retooling that would disciple him into self-referential stoic rationalism rather than a relationship with the living Savior. AJ could give Roger a course in basic Christian doctrines or a Navigators 2:7 study. In fact, AJ need not believe in counseling at all but might assert that sitting under the preaching of the Word and cultivating a more consistent devotional life will be sufficient to cure what ails Roger. Or AJ might seek to counsel Roger according to the principles and practices of some form of biblical counseling. In any case, it is *his* choice what sort of cure and care Roger will receive. AJ will not be taught, encouraged, or disciplined about that choice.

FIVE NEEDS

How can this problem be remedied? Let me identify five needs. First and foremost, Christian people (the church) need to become *wise in the face-to-face curing of souls*. We cannot articulate, practice, or regulate what we do not know how to do. Wisdom, love, and efficacy are highly attractive and persuasive. They adorn the truths that nourish them. But the church has been poor in understanding and enabling the processes of change, which makes the psychotherapies attractive to many. Wisdom must be conceptually articulate, methodologically skilled, and institutionally incarnated.

Let me highlight the institutional. *Who* will help troubled people? *Where* will that aid be found? *How long* will it last? *What forms* of help are offered? Because all ministry costs money, how will help be funded? The Bible's say on counseling will sound increasingly persuasive as mature biblical counseling characterizes the practice and structure of the church of Christ. Can we do what needs to be done?

Second, we need *creedal standards* for the curing of souls or at least a widely recognized body of practical theological writing. A system of practical theology serves as something to which we can refer and subscribe, towards which we can aim educationally, and from which we can be supervised and challenged regarding our faith and practice. A creed is a starting point for future development. It underscores the fact that everyone will approach counseling with some set of default beliefs that should be consciously examined and organized. Currently, the required "faith and practice" does not include views of counseling (except what can be derived from historical statements on the nature of ministry, human nature, and progressive sanctification). Faith and practice need to be extended into personality theory, counseling methodology, dynamics of change, and delivery systems for the curing of souls. What is the standard for faith and practice in counseling?

Third, we need *educational institutions* committed to the Bible's distinctive model of understanding persons and change. For many years, seminaries taught virtually nothing about progressive sanctification and the particulars of the curing of souls. In the past thirty years, there has been a stampede to create "counseling" programs, but the results are spotty in terms of consistent biblical thinking. Christian colleges typically contain a psychology department. But, typically, neither seminaries nor colleges teach things that significantly differ from what a secular institution would teach. Few teach how to counsel people in ways harmonious with the Bible's vision. How do people learn to become case-wise counselors?

Fourth, we need the curing of souls to be part of the church's *qualifying procedures* for trustworthy and skillful practitioners. Forms of recognizing truth, love, and skill need to be established at two levels. One level qualifies the pastoral leadership: licensure, ordination, accreditation, *per se*. Skill in counseling individuals, couples, and families must become as important a part of doctrinal faithfulness as skill in speaking to crowds. A second level of recognition qualifies church members to serve under the authority of pastor and elders. Here is where most counseling, formal or informal, will occur. Small group leaders, trained lay counselors, mentors, members who counsel in crisis pregnancy centers, and so forth, ought to operate within the unique Christian worldview. Most Christians who currently counsel with secular credentials are lay persons ecclesiastically, and they should submit their theories, methods, and structures to the church's oversight, subscribing to the distinctly Christian model of persons and change. How can wisdom and fidelity in conversational ministry be recognized and affirmed?

Fifth, we need ecclesiastically grounded *supervisory structures* for the curing of souls. The secular mental health professions usually offer continuing education, discipline for morals offenses, and case supervision to enhance skills and thinking. The church has often offered continuing education (books, seminars, D.Min. programs) and disciplined for morals or doctrinal offenses. But pastoral oversight – case supervision and discussion – are clear needs within local churches and elsewhere. There ought to be extensive interaction and supervision regarding the faith and practice of counseling. It *matters* what interpretations of life and advice are given to counselees. A secular psychotherapist can adopt any theoretical orientation – behavioral, cognitive, psychodynamic, existential, somatic, etc. – or can borrow from all of them and function multi-modally. The church does not believe in such theoretical diversity. It aims to refine its truth and love to reflect the way God sees things and the character and purposes of Jesus Christ, as revealed in the Bible. How can we protect and enhance counseling wisdom?

How Are We Doing?

How are we doing in this? Our current competencies, standards, structures, and functions are often far removed from what I am proposing. Perhaps it sounds ridiculous even to suggest that the church get a grip on the curing of souls. But without the Bible's wisdom on truth, practice, and the social structure of counseling and the church, the people of God do not really function as the people of God. The church *is* counsel and counseling if Ephesians 4 speaks truly. Life-changing truth and love is our calling.

The motivation theories of the modern psychologies would not last five minutes if they were examined in a decent systematic theology class on human nature. But the shoe fits on the other foot, too. The current state of most church structures, theoretical development, and counseling ministry practice would not last five minutes in a secular counseling class. The *Bible* gives us a social model; it is a seamless joining of specialized competency with community and peer resources, a seamless joining of nurturing and remedial functions, a seamless joining of comfort for those who suffer and transformation for those whose lives are malformed. But in the existing church, counselors and the community of care often fall woefully short of biblical standards.

We who call for the centrality of the church in counseling face a dilemma. The very thing we believe in lacks the necessary components to do the work. The shortcomings of secular psychotherapy are mirrored in the weaknesses among pastors and other Christian workers. It is fine to call Christians to pursue the curing of souls in submission to the local church. But the church needs to become a far better place for that to happen.

I believe that to organize counseling according to the mental health professional model is fundamentally, even disastrously, wrong. At the same time, truly wise church-oriented counseling ministry is decades away for the church as a whole. What must we do now? Jesus calls us to row in the right direction, however far away the destination seems. Let's aim right and work toward the right ends. Jesus Christ will complete us together in the maturity of his wisdom. Ephesians 4 gives our *modus operandi* as well as our goal. We are being redeemed. We must each labor to dismantle autonomous professionalism rather than reinforce it. We must each labor to make our loyalty to the church a significant reality rather than a mere statement of good intentions.

12 WHAT WILL YOU ASK FOR?

Let's say you've become convinced that biblical counseling should be a core ministry of the church of Christ. Where do you begin?

It's natural perhaps to think first of starting a formal counseling ministry or a training program for lay counselors, or of hiring a pastor who will specialize in pastoral care and the cure of souls. But let me suggest a humbler, simpler starting point. Take things that you and your church are already doing. For example, consider prayer or small groups or worship or premarital counseling or hospital visitation. Rethink the way you do these things. What are the implications of the fact that Jesus Christ is always "counseling" his beloved people? What are the implications of the fact that the Bible is always addressing the particulars of what people want, trust, fear, think, feel, and act? Take prayer, for example. Almost by definition, a church prays, a Christian prays. But how do we pray? What do we ask for? What do our prayers actually talk about? How does a counseling vision teach people a different way to make prayer requests? How does it change the way we pray?

Over the years, I've listened carefully to prayers. I've heard and participated in pastoral prayers, prayer meetings, small prayer groups, individual prayer requests. People tend to pray for predictable things. Among the most common:

- Heal the sick
- Comfort the bereaved

- Provide jobs and money to those in financial straits
- Bring family, friends, neighbors, and coworkers to faith in Jesus
- Help people to make major decisions wisely
- Protect those who are traveling
- Solve troubles and conflicts in family, work, school, and church
- Help us fulfill responsibilities on the job or in school
- Make ministries fruitful locally and around the world
- "Bless" and "be with" people, that good will happen

There's nothing wrong with asking for any of these things. They are good gifts. But notice something. None of them involve the sanctification and transformation of the one making the request or the one for whom you are praying. Such prayer requests ask for good gifts, but they do not ask for the best gift, that our lives would be remade into the image of Jesus.

What do you ask people to pray for? What do others ask you to pray for? It's as though we each look at life through a video camera and ask for changes in everything except the person filming. The cameraman is never in view. In other words, the "counseling" or "wisdom" needs of the person are rarely talked about. We will pray with parents for their straying teenager to straighten out; we rarely pray for the parents not to be fearful, bitter, passive or controlling. We will pray for a person to get a job; we rarely pray that he would grow in faith as he learns not to fret about money. We pray for the conversion of someone's loved ones; we rarely pray that the believer would grow more loving and honest in the way she treats those loved ones.

A biblical counseling vision will alter how you ask for prayer and how you pray. It is one of the simplest ways to start incorporating a biblical counseling vision into your life and ministry. As people learn to pray in a different way, they start to have reasons to counsel each other more meaningfully. They get in touch with the real battles. They increasingly enter into the primary lifelong calling to "be a disciple," a learner. A lifelong learner knows a profound need to give and receive counsel – every day (Heb. 3:12-14) – in order to grow up into the image of Jesus. As people become disciples, they increasingly understand their need for counsel. A church learning to pray rightly is a church taking a bold step toward becoming a community of mutual counsel.

Let's look at this through the particular example of praying for the sick. These are probably the most common prayer requests of all. I will frame the discussion from the standpoint of a pastor, who often invites and hears prayer requests, and often prays pastorally. The application to other problems and persons will be obvious.

* * *

How do you encourage members to pray beyond the sick list? This question has a simple answer but one that will keep all of us going for a long time: your members begin learning to pray beyond the sick list when *you* know how to pray beyond the sick list.

It sounds so simple. But it must not be that easy. Many pastoral prayers do not pray beyond the sick list – and they do not even pray very pointedly or intelligently for the sick. Many pastoral prayers sound like a nursing report at shift change in your local hospital: "The colon cancer in room 103 with uncertain prognosis . . . the broken leg that's mending well . . . the heart patient going into surgery . . . . " Such public prayers are often medically informative but spiritually impoverished. Usually physical healing is the sole goal.

DISHEARTENING PRAYERS

Visitors to many of our churches might be pardoned if they get the impression that God is chiefly interested in perking up our health, yet not very good at it! The prayer list in many churches is filled with chronic illnesses, though deep down we know that everyone will die sooner or later, usually from progressive ill health. Too often pastoral prayers, prayer meetings, and prayer lists dishearten and distract the faith of God's people. Prayer becomes either a dreary litany of familiar words, or a magical superstition. It either dulls our expectations of God, or hypes up fantasy hopes. Prayers for the sick can even become a breeding ground for cynicism: wouldn't these people have gotten better anyway as nature took its course or medicine succeeded? Prayer can also become a breeding ground for bizarre ideas and practices: a spiritualized version of our culture's obsession with health and medicine; naming and claiming your healing; a superstitious belief that the quantity or fervency of prayer is decisive in getting God's ear; the notion that prayer has its own "power"; questioning the faith of a person who doesn't get better.

It's hard to learn how to pray. It's hard enough for many of us to make an intelligent, honest request to friends we trust for something we truly need. And when the request is termed "praying" and the friend is termed "God," things get even more tangled. You've heard it the contorted syntax, formulaic phrases, meaningless repetition, vague non-requests, pious tone of voice, and air of confusion. If you talked to your friends or family that way, they'd think you'd lost your mind!

But if your understanding and practice of prayer changes, if your prayer requests and your model of prayer change, if your teaching on prayer changes, then you will change, and so will your relationship with God and his people.

Consider a few factors that can bring about such change.

LESSONS FROM JAMES'S PRAYERS FOR THE SICK

First, notice a few things about James 5:13-20. This passage is *the* warrant for praying for the sick. It is significant that James envisions prayer not in a congregational setting but in what we might think of as a counseling setting! The sick person asks for help, meets with a few elders, confesses sins, repents and draws near to God. Earnest prayer is described as affecting both the physical and spiritual states of that person. This doesn't mean it's wrong to pray from the pulpit for sick people. Of course not! But it ought to make us think twice that the classic text on praying for the sick assumes something highly personal and interpersonal taking place.

Notice how clearly James keeps spiritual issues in view. His letter is about growing in wisdom, and he doesn't change that emphasis when it comes to the sick. What he writes is based on his understanding that suffering is an occasion to become wise, a very good gift from above: "Consider it all joy, my brethren, when you meet various trials . . . . If any of you lacks wisdom, he should ask . . . . " (James 1:2, 5). He has already illustrated this regarding poverty, injustice, and interpersonal conflict. Now he illustrates it regarding sickness.

James's focus on the spiritual issues operating in suffering does not mean that people get sick because they've sinned. That's sometimes true: IV drug use and sexual immorality do lead to AIDS on occasion. People do reap in sickness what they sow in sin. But to make this into a universal rule is mere superstition or the heartlessness of Job's counselors.

At least two other dynamics also play out in the way God meets us in sickness. Sickness, like any other trouble, can force us to stop and face ourselves and find the Lord. I may find sins I've been too busy to notice: irritability, indifference, self-indulgence, unbelief, joylessness, worry, complaining, driven-ness, trust in my own health and ability. I may find my need for Jesus' mercies quickened and my delight in God deepened. I may develop fruit of the Spirit that can grow only by suffering well: endurance of faith; hope and joy that transcend circumstances; mature character; richer knowledge of God's love; living for God, not my pleasures; the humility of weakness; the ability to help others who suffer (James 1:3; Rom. 5:3-5; 1 Peter 1:6-8; 4:1-3; 2 Cor. 12:9-10; 1:4).

Sickness, like any trouble, is itself a temptation. Whether you face life-threatening disease or just feel lousy for a couple of days, it is amazing what that experience can bring out of your heart. Some people complain; others get angry – at God, at themselves, at others, at the inconvenience. Some pretend nothing's wrong; others pretend they're sicker than they are to get attention or avoid responsibilities. Some invest hope, time, and money in pursuing cure after cure. Others try to find someone or something to blame, even getting litigious. Still others just keep pressing on with life, doing, doing, doing – when God really intends them to stop and learn the lessons of weakness. Some become deeply fearful, imagining the worst. Some plunge into self-indulgence, manipulating everyone within reach to serve their every need. Others get depressed and question the value of their entire existence. Some are too proud to ask for help. Others brood that God must be out to get them, morbidly introspective about every real or imaginary failing.

You get the picture! Sickness provides one of the richest opportunities imaginable for spiritual growth and pastoral counseling, as James 5 makes clear. Is God interested in healing any particular illness? Sometimes. Is he always interested in making us wise, holy, trusting, and loving, even amid our pain, disability, and dying? Yes and amen.

People learn to pray beyond the sick list when they realize what God is really all about.

Three Kinds of Prayer

Second, consider the vast biblical teaching on prayer. How many of Scripture's prayers focus on sickness? A significant few, giving good reason to plead with God for healing. We've mentioned James 5. In Isaiah 38, Hezekiah pleads for restoration of health, and he is healed. In 2 Corinthians 12, Paul prays three times to be delivered from a painful affliction – but God said *No*. Psalm 35:12-14 mentions heartfelt prayer for the sick as a natural expression of loving concern. Both Elijah and Elisha plead to God for only sons whose deaths devastated their mothers (1 Kings 17; 2 Kings 4). In both cases God restores them. Coming at the issue from the opposite direction, the Bible's last word on Asa is negative because "his disease was severe, yet even in his disease he did not seek the Lord, but the physicians" (2 Chron. 16:12).

Prayer has many degrees of intensity, with supplication and outcry the strongest. It is striking how passionate and blunt the prayers for healing are. These passages vividly challenge the perfunctory prayers that often are offered even by people preoccupied with illness! When you pray for the sick (or teach the sick to seek God themselves), it ought to be a fiercely thoughtful firestorm.

It is clear, however, that the vast majority of Scriptural prayers focus on other things. Broadly speaking, there are three emphases of biblical prayer: circumstantial prayers, wisdom prayers, and kingdom prayers. Praying for the sick is a form of the first.

- Sometimes we ask God to *change our circumstances:* heal the sick, give daily bread, protect from suffering and evil, make our leaders just, convert friends and family, make our work prosper, provide me with a spouse, quiet this storm, send rain, give us a child.
- Sometimes we ask God to *change us:* deepen my faith, teach us to love each other, forgive sins, make me wise, make us know you better, help me to sanctify you in my heart, don't let me dishonor you, help us understand Scripture, teach me to encourage others.
- Sometimes we ask God to *change everything by revealing himself* more fully, magnifying his glory and rule. Your kingdom come, your will be done on earth as it is in heaven, be exalted above the heavens, let your glory be over all of the earth, come Lord Jesus.

In the Lord's Prayer you see examples of all three, tightly interwoven. The Lord's kingdom involves the destruction of our sins and sufferings. His reign causes a flourishing of love's wisdom and a wealth of situational blessing. Prayers for God to change me and my circumstances are requests that he reveal his glory and mercy on the stage of this world.

When any of these three gets detached from the other two, prayer tends to go sour. If you just pray for better circumstances, God becomes the errand boy (usually disappointing) who exists to fill your shopping list of desires – no sanctifying purposes, no higher glory. If you only pray for personal change, it tends to reveal an obsession with moral self-improvement, a self-absorbed spirituality detached from others and the tasks of life. Where is the longing for Christ's kingdom to right *all* wrongs, not just to alleviate my sins so I don't feel bad about myself? If you only pray for the sweeping invasion of the kingdom, prayers are over-generalized, failing to walk out how the kingdom rights real wrongs, wipes away real tears, and removes real sins. Prayer pursues a God who never touches ground until the last day.

We could give countless examples of these three sorts of prayer. Consider the Psalms, *the* book of talking with God. About ninety psalms are "minor key." Intercessions regarding sin and suffering predominate – always in light of God revealing his mercies, power, and kingdom. In about one-third of these, the battle with personal sin and guilt appears. Often there are requests that God make us wiser: "Teach me"; "Give me understanding"; "Revive me." In many more psalms, you see requests to change circumstances: deliver me from evildoers; be my refuge and fortress; destroy your enemies. These are always tied to requests that God arrive with kingdom glory and power. God reveals himself by making these bad things and bad people go away! Then there are the sixty or so "major key" psalms. These emphasize the joy and praise that mark God's kingdom reign revealed.

Consider also the prayers of Philippians 1:9-11 and Colossians 1:9-14. Here we see no mention of circumstances, no request to be healed, fed, or protected. The requests focus on gaining wisdom (in light of the coming of God's kingdom). Such wisdom expresses itself in vertical and horizontal dimensions, love for God and love for neighbor. These two prayers plead with God to deepen both kinds of love in others: may God make you know him better. May God make your love for people wise.

Finally, consider Ephesians 1:15-23 and 3:14-21. Here, too, the prayers focus on wisdom in light of Christ's glory. Again, there are no circumstantial requests; there aren't even requests to grow in intelligent love for others. Paul zeroes in what we need most: that God would make you know him better.

Why don't people pray beyond the sick list? We pray for circumstances to improve so that we might feel better and life might get better. These are often honest and good requests – unless they're the only requests we make. Detached from the purposes of sanctification and a yearning for the coming of the King, prayers for circumstances become self-centered.

Teach people to pray with the three-stranded braid of our real need. They will pray far beyond the sick list. And they will pray in a noticeably different way for the sick. They won't just be praying for alleviation of the troubles of life. They will be praying for the things that counseling is about: transforming decision makers who live in the midst of those troubles.

13   Pastoral Counseling

What percentage of time should a pastor give to counseling? This question has no one-size-fits-all answer. God never clones the snowflakes in his blizzards. Surely he never clones the servants in his church! Differences of calling are shaped by many factors: patterns of personal and congregational gifting, interests and desires, life experience and maturity, staffing and job description, demographics of congregational and community need, and so forth. Some pastors will dedicate a significant portion of their week to various forms of *interpersonal or conversational ministry* (i.e., counseling). Others will give more of their time and attention to public ministries, to diaconal and mercy ministries, or to administrative and infrastructure ministries.

Public and Interpersonal Ministry

The distinction between public ministry and interpersonal ministry is important for answering the question. Both work directly with the Word. You must know God's ways and will. Both work directly with people. You must know people. Both bring grace and truth to renovate lives. Both call a pastor to live what he says. Both call for creativity in application. There is a fundamental overlap of intention and content. But there are some key differences in method. Every word out of your mouth ought to be grace-giving – but what gets said comes out in quite a different way during the dialogue of conversation than during the monologue of a public address.

Public ministries include worship, preaching, teaching, sacraments, corporate prayer, and modeling. These apply truth generally. No one is named; no one's specific struggles are mentioned; no one's exact life situation is pointed out. The pastor never says, "Hephzibah Jones, there in the third row, you're struggling because your husband Hezekiah is indifferent and harsh towards you. Zi, you're tempted to be bitter, fearful, and to think that God has forgotten you. Zeke, you use her bitterness as an excuse for your wrongs against her. But it says here in Psalm 31 that . . . . " That's not how to do it! And we instinctively know that.

Instead the Holy Spirit takes truth exposited from, say, Psalm 31 that we apply either in general or with other people's stories (people from history, Scripture, film, literature, or from the preacher's own life). God does the personalizing, making truth relevant and nourishing within the hearts of Zi, Zeke, and all others present. In public ministry the minister doesn't necessarily even know the names of all those to whom he ministers. Hearers may know next to nothing about the speaker and still profit. And public ministry is generally planned and scripted to a significant degree. You usually have time to prepare and a pretty good idea what you're going to say and do.

Interpersonal ministries are different. They include discipleship, visitation, mentoring, pastoral counseling, conciliation, one-anothering, intentional friendship, small group leadership, casual conversation, child rearing, and church discipline. These apply truth to the particular needs of particular people. You'd better know people's names (and lots of other details) in conversational ministry! You talk directly with Zi and Zeke. You ask questions. You listen and express concern. You share who you are and draw out their questions. You say a couple of sentences, or tell a story, or give a brief teaching or encouragement, and then get their response. It's a continual give and take as you work together to come to understanding and make application. You don't know Zi's next sentence, so you don't know yours! Conversation is an improvisation controlled by the goal of speaking the truth in love. Skills in interaction are essential.

Two Rules of Thumb

All this said, let me give my two-fold rule of thumb about the place of counseling in a pastor's week. *Every pastor ought to dedicate some percentage of his ministry to counseling conversations. Every pastor ought to be meeting with one or two people who are slow movers.*

First, *every* pastor ought to do *some* counseling. Talking with people is the best way to measure the pulpit ministry's effectiveness. Does what you know, believe, and preach actually help people? Talking one to one about what matters in life is the only way you'll ever really get to know people. And knowing people is the only way you'll ever learn to preach to them. Is the truth you know good enough for crowds on Sunday morning but not good enough for individual strugglers on Tuesday afternoon? If so, it's not good enough.

I've often heard "ministry of the Word" equated with "the pulpit." One sometimes gets an idealized image of the preaching pastor as a man who moves from the contemplation of his study to the proclamation of his pulpit without ever needing the messiness of life to sully his message! This is surely a false ideal of biblical ministry. We need only consider that the majority of our Lord's ministry was conversational, asking and answering questions, and responding to interruptions. We need only consider the prominence in the Bible of one-anothering, the tongue, and the interpersonal immediacy of love. These are the proofs that our faith is real. The pastor had better take the lead as someone living in reality, not religious fantasy.

As a minimum, consider marking out one afternoon a week for significant, intentional conversations. (That's not even considering that *every* interaction ought to provide a small counseling moment where your interest and your words can be grace-giving.) That conversational ministry will keep you honest and make you wise. You'll be able to field test whether what you said last Sunday really flies. What you say next Sunday will be better, more timely, more realistic, and more practical. You'll learn how change actually occurs, the fits and starts, the genuine progress, the pitfalls and regressions.

I've too often heard it said, "Just preach the Word faithfully and teach people how to meet the Lord on their own, and you won't need to counsel." I view this statement as close to pernicious. It contains a sweet half-truth: good preaching and devotional life *do* help people avoid many problems. They *do* enable people to solve existing problems so that a counseling appointment isn't needed. But the statement gets its conclusion exactly backwards. If Ephesians 4 and Hebrews 3:12-14 are true, then "Preach the Word faithfully and teach people how to meet the Lord on their own, and you'll create *a community of wise mutual counseling.*" The pastor of the sheep (himself a sheep of the Pastor) ought to be an example of speaking the truth in love. This is the prime characteristic of wise mutual counseling and the prime characteristic of a working community in Christ.

My second rule of thumb is perhaps more controversial. You should always be involved with a few people who are slow movers, with strugglers. The temptation is to counsel leader types, gifted people who want to grow. People who are a quick study. People who get it. Educated, independent, competent people. Influential people. Such people often make for efficient counseling (though not necessarily). They might not need more than a consultation or two. It doesn't necessarily require you to deal with the confusion, willfulness, and suffering of the human heart. But sheep *are* often needy, confused, broken, harassed, stubborn, fearful, slow to grow, and forgetful. They are really just like pastors and other leaders, however much the ideals of our own competency can beguile us!

Hebrews 5:2-3 provides one of the most challenging descriptions of ministry imaginable. The wise priest "can deal gently with the ignorant and misguided, since he himself also is beset with weakness; and because of it he is obligated to offer sacrifices for sins, as for the people, so also for himself." Ignorant: they don't get it. Misguided: they stray. Weakness: fundamental inability, disability, and liability. And then this: Deal gently with the slow movers and strugglers, with those whose troubles and failings overwhelm them.

Of course, you can't counsel twenty such people every week. You aren't in the business of making anyone dependent on you. You aren't the Messiah. There are times you must say fish or cut bait, and let's quit wasting time. And much of the discipleship and counseling you do ought to equip gifted people to help carry their share of ministry.

BLESSED ARE THE POOR IN SPIRIT

But all that said, I have found that the slow-movers have taught me the most about myself, about God's mercy, and about how to love. You can't get away with a pat answer, a formula, a pet doctrine, a quick fix. You learn that people rarely change and grow just because you said a wise word once.

I enjoy being a consultant on a person's life. I enjoy being able to offer crisp biblical analysis of what's going on and to propose clear biblical solutions. But I had to learn how to love. I had to learn patience. I had to learn to weep with those who weep. I had to learn how to build trust and the genuine honesty that flourishes only within trust. I had to learn how to go over the same ground yet again, in a slightly different way, and never lose hope, and never lose freshness. I had to learn how Jesus loves the less presentable members of his body, and how the Lord bears with us all – one of his most outstanding (and least recognized) characteristics.

I had to learn over and over that grace flows downhill to the needy and troubled. I had to learn that "Blessed are the poor in spirit" (Matt 5:3) is not only the *first* beatitude – as if one might master step one and then move on to steps two and three! It is the *foundational* beatitude. You build everything else on that foundation.

Our fundamental need for mercy never goes away. If you remain alive to your need for Jesus' redemption, you learn to take this to heart more and more. I had to learn how to deal gently and persistently with the ignorant and misguided, with the confused and beaten down, with the inept and suspicious. I had to learn that "admonish the unruly" is followed by "encourage the faint-hearted; hold onto the weak; be patient with them all" (1 Thess. 5:14). I had to learn how love must confirm our words about the love of God in Christ. I'm still learning. And I am so grateful that Jesus deals gently with me.

The slow movers Jesus loves . . . I am one of them. It makes me face our collective need. Jesus must redeem all of us together.

Steadily counseling a few slow movers will help take out of your ministry any slickness, any pompousness, any pat answers, any posturing, any pretending, any self-righteousness, any doing it just for the successful results. It will make your people know you care . . . because you do.

What percentage of time should a pastor give to counseling? Some percentage. And make sure that some percent of that percentage is given to people who will never be leaders. Then again, God may surprise you. Those one-time slow movers may someday prove to be in the front lines of your church's patient, tenderhearted counseling ministry to other strugglers. They learned it somewhere – from you.

14 COUNSELING UNDER THE INFLUENCE OF THE X CHROMOSOME

When we think about counseling and discipleship within the body of Christ, we inevitably must consider women who counsel and who seek to counsel in fidelity to Christ's word of grace and truth.

Doing so does not thrust us into the world's debate on male and female. The God who made us male and female manages to avoid both masculinist and feminist extremes. His design calls forth neither tyranny nor anarchy, monarchy nor democracy, traditionalism nor egalitarianism. Submission to Christ is a different dance step altogether. There are issues in counseling with implications for how male and female serve Christ fruitfully, but the fact that Jesus Christ populates his church with wise female counselors teaches us much about *how* we live out both the common and the complementary in his design.

UNIVERSAL YET DISTINCT

Moreover, there are few issues in counseling that are the exclusive domain of women. A crisis pregnancy is an essentially female topic, but the immoralities that usually precede such pregnancies implicate both sexes. Most of what women and men deal with is generically the same. Both male and female sin in the same basic ways. Complaining, worry, resentment, unbelief, and self-righteousness are gender-blind. And both male and female suffer life's pains and hardships, so Christ's mercies come to both. Faith works through love in both. Both sexes apply psalms, most proverbs, the Sermon on the Mount, John, and most of Ephesians 4-6 in the same ways.

Often idiosyncratic differences between individuals have more impact than supposed gender differences. Some men come from Venus and some women from Mars. Some women are natural initiators, while some men are instinctive responders. Some men are nurturers and some women are achievers. Some women love to balance the checkbook, some men love to cook, and so on. Generalizations don't work as absolutes.

Even problems once said to be typically male or female aren't set in stone. Troubles with body image, depression, and being abused were once distinctively female. But eating disorders, obsession with appearance, hopelessness, and the experience of violation are increasingly male. Pornography, lewdness, violent behavior, and foul language were once characteristically male evils. They are increasingly female.

Thus the most significant things about *people* are universal. Having said that, however, your sex and gender (female/male biologically and feminine/masculine culturally) always give things a particular spin. When what's universally human is expressed with a woman's sensibility, it's a bit different. This is analogous to issues in a cross-cultural or cross-situational ministry. The one Christ engages every nation, tribe, tongue, and people – male and female – without homogenizing us. A converted peasant woman in Uttar Pradesh is somehow different from a California dotcom executive who came to Christ when the bubble burst. They are significantly different yet fundamentally the same. So women are different from men, and *vive la différence!* Yet no temptation has overtaken you that is not common to all, and we all grow up into the image of Jesus.

FOUR OBSERVATIONS

Experience and reflection in these matters leads me to make four observations. First, I've been teaching counseling at Westminster Seminary since 1980. I've taught over 1500 students, evenly divided between males and females. Half the time, the top student in the class has been female. Male or female has never correlated either to the top or bottom half of the class. I suspect that this is because counseling wisdom is an exquisite mix of three things:

- a personal integrity that applies the truth firsthand (humility)
- a breadth and depth of knowledge, of God and people (truth)
- a rich bundle of relational skills and attitudes (love).

God is no respecter of persons when he weaves such wisdom into the fabric of our souls. Some male seminarians who do well in more technical academic courses do relatively poorly in counseling classes. Their grasp of truth is systematic and articulate but overly theoretical and depersonalized. They don't bring the Bible to life (in both senses). They lack the ability to *apply* it to themselves and others. Women often personalize truth to themselves and others with cogency, candor, and subtlety. Yes, some women are theoretical, while some men are fine personalizers of truth. But God seems to level the playing field when imparting wisdom for the tasks of mutual ministry.

Second, one evening recently we hosted a group of women for a discussion in our home. Nancy Leigh DeMoss (author and host of the radio show "Revive our Hearts") met with eight female counselors from CCEF. I was the token male. Nancy wanted to consider how to address the deep life problems of women who call or write in for help.

It was fascinating to be a fly on the wall. The *way* these women discussed things was distinctively different from the way a group of nine men might talk about cases and problems. It was not a difference of worldview, counseling model, or theological perspective. All the same life problems and theological perspectives were on the table: the sovereign immediacy of God's purposes working in people's lives, the dynamics of change, the character of indwelling sin, the experience of suffering, the operations of grace, the role of the counselor as a speaker of truth in love, the 2 Corinthians 1:4 and 1 Corinthians 10:13 dynamics that connect one's own story to the stories of others, the principles of wise obedience outworking into particular situations. These things were always present but usually implicit.

The three-hour discussion was woven from personal experiences, counseling anecdotes, and stories about how Christ's grace and truth met *this* woman in *those* sufferings and *these* sins. Often someone began by saying, "In my own life, when. . . . " This is not because these women were self-centered or didn't care about the Bible's authority. On the contrary! What happened in our living room was much like counseling itself: multi-stranded story more than single-stranded topic. In fact, it was like most of the Bible. Life lived was out on the table, to be met by God. The bones and muscles of Scripture and theology gave underlying shape and power to what each woman knew, felt, said, and did, but the stories were what you saw and heard most clearly.

Third, it is surely significant that the vast majority of promises, commands, stories, and revelations of God in the Bible are not gender specific. Women learn from Joseph's tender heart; men learn from Esther's courage. In the same way, most of Scripture is not exclusively addressed to any particular age group, ethnic background, marital status, socioeconomic level, role in the church, or life experience. The general call of God's revelation crosses lines to shine one light into all darkness. Your sex neither privileges nor disadvantages you. The Maker of heaven and earth watches over each and all. He calls all into relationship with Christ. When he says, "The tongue of the wise is a tree of life," the giver of such wisdom might be a Josefina or a Joseph, Norwegian or Nigerian, aged or teenaged, former Hell's Angel or formerly angelic Pollyanna.

This is not to make differences irrelevant. Scripture often helps us to get pointedly personal by applying universal promises and general directives: "to the unmarried . . . wives . . . husbands . . . children . . . fathers . . . elders . . . young men . . . younger widows . . . older men . . . older women . . . is anyone suffering? . . . is anyone cheerful? . . . to the poor . . . to the rich . . . masters . . . servants . . . we who are Jews . . . you gentiles." We who now apply God's Word always personalize truth with our own stories. We are his workmanship, and this master craftsman and artist never does it the same way twice.

When the Ten Commandments get posted on a courthouse wall or rehearsed in Sunday school, they might sound like a list of timeless dos and don'ts. But God's actual "ten words" burst with timely specifics. He revealed his name and relationship (YHWH your God), his character (jealous and loving), his actions (maker of all that is, who has saved you, and will either save or destroy), and his will (those ten commands unfolding the nature of love for God and others). These ten words about God and love came originally packaged with many particulars: to an ethnic group with its immediate history (Ex. 20:2), planted amid idol-makers (20:4), operating on a household economy (20:10), whose children would soon live in the hills and plains of Canaan (20:12), whose possessions and social structure characterized an ancient Near Eastern agrarian society (20:17).

Theological shorthand neuters the Bible of persons, places, and experiences to extract the abiding principles and propositions. Life application always resexes the truth; that is, counseling puts the personal details back in. It matters whether you are male or female. Are you elderly, in the prime of life, or young? It matters. Are you Korean, Honduran, or German? Single, married, widowed, or divorced? Parent or child? Wealthy or living hand-to-mouth? Frail or robust? Pastor or new believer? Recipient of serving gifts or verbal gifts? We are to count it joy when we face "various trials" (James 1:2): what sort uniquely stamps you?

Counseling, like Scripture, comes to life in the differences that make every story unique. On the one hand, John writes, "There are also many other things which Jesus did, which if they were written in detail, I suppose that even the world itself would not contain the books that would be written" (John 21:25). On the other hand, those countless books are still being written by the Spirit of God on the pages of our hearts. Each book tells a different story; all the books tell the same story. Most of the Bible is not gender-specific, but none of it is gender-neutral. God meets people who are male or female.

Finally, biblical counseling as a social movement over the

past thirty years or so has had a strongly "masculine" feel. That's understandable for a number of reasons. First, the original impetus was to call biblically oriented pastors to step up to their counseling responsibilities rather than defer to mental health professionals. Second, a commitment to Scripture usually correlates with a desire to raise up men after God's own heart, teachable and loving, willing to lead in home and church life. Third, when counseling is committed to church discipline for high-handed sin, it spotlights situations where love must speak bluntly and take authoritative action.

But some reasons for the masculine feel to the biblical counseling movement call for midcourse corrections. Good things need to be complemented by other good things for the sake of breadth, balance, and beauty. Good pastoral theology is always a work in progress, both a product and a producer of the endless conversation by which we, the church, grow up.

CONTRIBUTIONS TO WISDOM

In the providence of God, interest in biblical counseling among women is exploding. It's no accident that females compose half (or more) of the thousands of students and practitioners of biblical counseling. That brings *la différence* more to the fore, brings different truths, graces, and needs into clearer view, and bids to make what is held in common richer and deeper. God uses the gifts and perspectives of women to bless other women *and* men. Women rightly want a mature, biblical wisdom that maps onto their life experiences, ministry opportunities, and patterns of constructive relationship. And these concerns, I submit, lead them to make these contributions to the maturing of our collective wisdom:

- Wisdom often speaks in stories and experience as well as in theological propositions and ethical principles. Human life unfolds like Scripture, a living story about people with names living in places, facing troubles, experiencing joys, voicing hopes and fears immediate to each situation.
- Wisdom often speaks from within the one-anothering

stance of mutual relationship as well as from the authoritative stance of designated teacher with responsible oversight. Every one of us is sheep, child, servant, wife, foot soldier, student, and friend with respect to the Lord.

- Wisdom often speaks the language of refuge, comforting and protecting sufferers as well as the language of mercy and power to transform sinners. The "weakness" that the Spirit aids (Rom. 8:26), about which psalms cry out and Jesus sympathizes (Heb. 4:15), encompasses the whole human condition.

- Wisdom speaks considerately, respecting the feelings of others, affirming and nourishing even small goods as well as frankly addressing what is still wrong. An evident patience and kindness – love's leading attribute – pays close attention to the qualities of gracious relationship that give every word its context, tone, and connotation.

What makes women's counseling worthy of the adjectives "Christian" and "biblical"? The same things as men's counseling. It's surely not that the one leading in the conversation happens to profess personal faith in Jesus Christ. It's surely not that Bible verses get talked about, or that Jesus is mentioned, or that prayer happens. It surely is what one woman who counsels calls "private lessons in applied theology." Everything then hangs on the *quality* of what happens in private: the quality of the mercies shown, the quality of the knowledge gained, the quality of the theology brought to bear, the quality of the applications made.

15   DO YOU EVER REFER?

This book makes the case that counseling is properly a core ministry of the church of Jesus Christ. That naturally raises the question of whether or not to refer to mental health professionals. Let me first come at this question from what might seem like an odd angle, by addressing a similar question: *Do you ever refer people to pastors or other pastoral counselors for help?* Would I suggest that someone attend church? Sit under preaching? Join in worship? Build friendships? Seek personal counsel? Whether public or private, formal or informal, each of these is "counseling." Each communicates a framework of meaning in the context of relationship. For good or ill, each shapes a person's worldview, identity, values, choices, and emotional reactions. So should you ever refer a person you love to a church for help?

A. Of course

B. Never

C. It depends

My answer is C. It depends.

What does it depend on? It depends on the quality of truth and love in that community of counselors. I would never say, "You need to go to a church. Go talk to a pastor." That would be irresponsible, even dangerous. What if the "truth" is false? What if the "love" is a sham? Instead, I would always want to know, "What kind of church is this? Who is this pastor? What do they believe, and how do they practice?" All counselors lead or mislead, guide or misguide, reform or deform those they form. Does this particular counselor embody and speak what is necessary to care for my friend's soul? That's not answered by a job title, such as "pastor" or "counselor." In Paul's words from 1 Timothy 4:16, it depends on the counselor's "doctrine and life." My decision to refer to pastors or pastoral counselors is not based on anyone's title, but on three, more substantial matters: What do you say you believe? What do you show you believe? How do you treat other people?

THREE KEY QUESTIONS

First, what are a counselor's *professed* views of human nature, motivation, the change process, the causes of problems, the influence of suffering and social factors? What do you say you believe about the place of Scripture to understand and help people, the role of Jesus Christ, the Holy Spirit, and the Father in changing us, and so forth? Every counseling model – secular or Christian – holds an explicit or implicit view on each of these questions. Because the all-wise God holds an explicit view, I want my friend to talk with someone who will express (more rather than less – none of us gets it perfect) God's merciful wisdom. What if a pastor believes that childhood upbringing, low self-esteem, genetics, or an unmet love need is the cause of our problems? What if a pastor believes that one particular doctrine, experience, or strategy will solve a person's problems once and for all? In either case, no referral! My friend will not be helped by a deterministic theory or a quick fix.

Second, what is this counselor's *functional* answer to those same questions? What emphases actually come out in counseling conversations? What outlook determines the questions asked, the interpretations offered, the interventions and suggestions? What if a pastor states that God's relationship with us is sustained by his gracious purposes, but in practice his counsel consists entirely of communication tips, planning strategies, dos and don'ts, and exhortations to try harder? What if a pastoral counselor claims to deal biblically with sin, suffering, and redemption, but in practice winds up sounding like a pop psychologist? No referral. My friend will not be changed by what is offered.

So far, we've asked questions about "doctrine." Third, just as important, there are questions about the pastoral counselor's "life." What kind of person are you? How do you treat people? What attitudes come through? Would I trust you in talking through my own struggles? Would I entrust someone I love to your care, confident that truth will come wrapped in love? A decision to refer must reflect a positive assessment of the counselor's personal character, breadth of experience with people, scope of wisdom, patience, kindness, courage, humility, gentleness, perceptiveness, directness, reputation for helpfulness, judiciousness, maturity, and the like. What if a pastor comes across as arrogant, with a sure cure for all that ails you? What if he comes across as timid, ready to say whatever is agreeable? In either case, no referral.

All these assessments contribute to the degree of confidence I will have. Think about the bottom line: To "refer for counseling" means to entrust a person I love into the hands of a person I trust. Where does trust come from? The counselor's title and education mean relatively little. Instead, who is this counselor as a person? What does this counselor really believe when it comes to making sense of life's troubles and restoring a soul? How does this counselor treat people? These matters of wisdom prove decisive in determining whether to refer.

DOCTRINE, LIFE, AND LABEL

Now let's return to our original question: *Do you ever refer people to psychologists or psychiatrists for help?* I offer the exact same answer. It depends. And it depends on exactly the same factors (with a few wrinkles I'll mention later).

The decisive question when it comes to counseling help is not professional title or education, but "doctrine and life." If the person with a mental health title is committed to a biblical vision of persons and change, then the professional title is incidental.[1] A label means far less than what is within the person. But when it comes to psychotherapists, this fact is often ignored. Many people are discerning about the label "pastor" and would never refer a friend for help unless they were confident that the pastor's doctrine and life consistently reflected Christ. But those same people will often take at face value the labels "psychologist," "psychiatrist," and "counselor," relying on credentials to confer objective, neutral, scientific expertise.

But all counseling, even so-called "non-directive" counseling, is value-laden. In counseling one person aims to explore, reinterpret, and redirect another person's life. Every counselor sizes up the reasons for another person's troubles, weighing his or her emotions, actions, and thoughts against interpretive criteria. Every counselor operates within a framework of meaning. Every counselor seeks to elicit trust. Every counselor wants facts: what happened to you, how you're reacting, what you're thinking, what you think would help, etc. Whether you are talking to "a professional" or to your mother, that person will propose (explicitly or implicitly) some way of (re)interpreting your life experience. That counselor will then suggest or imply some path of action or altered response. In other words, all counseling conversations aim at the "care and cure of souls."

But counselors define what's wrong and what makes it right a thousand different ways. Every word that every counselor says (or doesn't say) teaches a particular way of seeing and explaining life. Every follow-up question follows a line of reasoning arising from that counselor's particular way of interpreting life. The bottom line? Psychotherapists, like pastors, come prepared to lead you in a particular direction. You'd better get behind the label to weigh "doctrine and life" seriously.

When it comes to counseling, I will only refer to someone whose way of helping corresponds (more, not less) to biblical wisdom. Jesus Christ is in the business of remaking lives that express more faith and more love. Counseling is only wise when it is in the same business.

OTHER HELPFUL SKILLS

The vast majority of psychiatrists and psychologists do not consciously practice within a God-centered universe where a Redeemer works to deliver us from our self-centeredness. But here's another significant question: Would I ever refer to such professionals for reasons besides counseling? Yes, of course. Some of their skills can prove very helpful, particularly in assessment. A psychiatrist's medical training can help determine whether a neurological or other organic factor contributes to a person's problems. Is there an identifiable dysfunction or disability linked to thyroid, neurological problems, medications, brain tumor, Alzheimer's, concussion, etc.?[2] Of course, a psychiatrist might describe that biological factor as the only significant factor rather than one of many. But we can sift out the overstatement and still profit from the diagnosis and (where possible) the treatment of a physical ailment.

In a similar way, a psychologist might help by providing an assessment of mental status and psychological functioning. Is this person disoriented? Controlled by bizarre ideas? A psychologist might perform and interpret intelligence and other aptitude tests: What abilities and limitations affect this person's options regarding education, job, etc.? Perhaps a psychologist is experienced in the struggles of adopted children – "attachment disorders." That expertise could prove informative to parents, allaying fears, adjusting expectations about the future, and identifying options available to help the child.

None of these assessments is "neutral-objective," of course. The presentation and interpretation of data always come with worldview and values attached. That worldview may miss or distort significant factors. For example, it makes a difference whether or not you interpret "abilities" and "disabilities" as gifts of God. The more able are humbled by their endowments. The more disabled are dignified in their limitations. Down's Syndrome, Asperger Syndrome, and other "disabilities" occur within the providence of God (Ex. 4:11). One interpretation may portray such biological factors in an overly determinative way, blinding us to the normal human struggles these individuals experience. Another interpretation may portray social factors in an overly determinative way. For example, some adopted children experience a typical cluster of struggles. But these children are not *determined* by their past social experiences any more than they are by their genetics.

The motives of every child's heart intersect with every

experience, every ability or disability, every opportunity or limitation. That's Biblical Worldview 101. It's God's worldview. It's how reality works. James 1:13-16, for example, was written to people who were uprooted by immigration, degraded by economic oppression, left vulnerable and helpless by being widowed or orphaned, and inflamed with interpersonal conflicts. The social experience is significant and influential. It sets the stage on which we live. But it is not deterministic. The experiences of adopted children or highly distractible children are variants on normal human experience. They are not uniquely soul-disfiguring forms of suffering. You will always have to size up the facts, diagnoses, and advice that a psychologist offers. But all that information can still be helpful.

THE BELIEVING PSYCHOTHERAPIST

Here's another question. What if a psychotherapist is a believing Christian? Doesn't that make a difference? We've already mentioned that the key is not job title or educational credentials, but actual wisdom faithful to God's stated intentions and point of view. If a Christian psychotherapist practices true to Christian faith, then he or she does nothing essentially different from a wise parent, friend, pastor, or other counselor who counsels and lives true to the Christian faith. But in my observation, professional practice rarely connects very well with professed beliefs and personal ethics. Psychotherapists whose personal faith is admirable typically counsel from a different perspective than what their faith professes.

Why is this so? Why, for example, the preponderance among evangelical psychotherapists of need theory, personal history determinism, temperament theory, cognitive-behavioral methodology, and a "professional" ideology of counseling practice? Here are two significant reasons, one obvious, one deeply buried. The obvious reason is that they haven't rethought the categories of thought they absorbed in professional education. One of the oldest self-criticisms among Christian psychotherapists is that they know grad school psychology and Sunday school theology. The dots don't connect between God and real life, so the theology is relatively irrelevant to daily life problems.

The less obvious reason is deeper. There is a built-in pressure on Christians who are psychologists to deviate from Scripture. How else can they define themselves as legitimate professionals possessing some unique knowledge base and expertise? Because the Bible says so much about people's problems and counseling, it means that biblical wisdom is common property. The Word lies open to all, and the Spirit is freely given to write God's point of view on hearts. The territory that psychologists claim is not theirs by natural right. Life's sufferings, unruly emotions, broken relationships, addictions, distorted thinking, and the rest are what the Bible is about. That's common property humanity. That's what God's redeeming love and truth hold in view.

As a human being, a psychotherapist may be wise or foolish in addressing life's problems. As mental health professionals, they don't own the interpretation of, or the solution to, those problems. These same problems are the territory of a host of practical advisers who make no pretense to being psychologists. From the years I worked in psychiatric hospitals, I'll never forget how our down-to-earth, caring housekeeper had the greatest positive influence on a number of patients!

Evangelicals doing psychotherapy almost invariably justify what they do as something qualitatively different from wise friendship and good pastoral counseling. *Professional* identity depends on possessing some unique area of knowledge and skill. How is this different from practical truth, genuine love, wide-ranging knowledge, and wisdom about all that pertains to being human (each in the biblical sense!)? The professional claim to unique expertise does not hold up under examination. A non-psychologist is often more insightful and helpful than a psychotherapist. The problems psychologists address are the same ones the Bible addresses. Claims to professional prerogatives do not necessarily overlap with biblical wisdom.

ASSESSING PSYCHOLOGY'S CLAIMS

Consider one example of how professional self-justification overrides the deeper implications of Christian thinking about the mental health professions. Many years ago I received the following letter from an evangelical organization promoting the role of Christian psychologists.

> Psychologists do far more than engage in the practice of psychotherapy. To whom would you take a six-year-old boy to determine whether he was emotionally and physically ready to enter first grade? To whom would you turn if your wife became schizophrenic and ran screaming down the street? Would your pastor be able to deal with that situation? What if you wished to make a career change . . . and wanted an objective evaluation of your strengths and interests? Whom could you ask to help you? To whom would you go to seek help with an adolescent who was extremely rebellious and resentful of his father? In each of these instances, and in a hundred others, you should look for a psychologist whose first love and highest commitment is to Jesus Christ and to the Word of God. And how silly to say, "There is no such thing."[3]

It's a fascinating letter. Let's analyze the rhetorical strategy. For starters, I would certainly agree that it is silly to say, "There is no such thing." I know a number of "psychologists" who not only make Jesus and the Word their first love and highest commitment, but (more significantly) they apply that commitment to the details of how they understand people and practice counseling. They are biblical counselors in the content and method of their counseling, though they have another career title (psychotherapist) appended to their name. There are wildly different psychotherapy systems that make no reference to biblical realities – family systems, cognitive-behavioral, Gestalt, Freudian, etc. There is no reason there can't be a coherently Christian "psychotherapist" – a biblical counselor, in other words. But such coherence between first love and the details of model and practice is unusual.

A Closer Look

Let's ponder this letter in more detail. First, it is interesting how assessment roles (school readiness, career aptitude) and counseling roles (disturbed wife, hostile adolescent) are carefully intermingled. Those are very different things (and rarely coexist in the same counselor). Second, it is interesting how the psychotherapy role itself is downplayed. That role – along with theories of human personality that inhabit therapy models – is exactly what is controversial. Third, it is interesting that attention focuses entirely on "social roles" that seem like givens in the professional landscape of American society. No mention is made of the many ideas-doctrines-teachings that psychologists have mediated straight from secular personality theories into the church. Fourth, it is also interesting how pastors, family, and friends are presumably incompetent for counseling situations (or even to play a role in assessment, though they may know the person best). There is even one direct swipe at the church: "Would your pastor know how to deal with this?" Of course, *your* pastor might not know how, but not all pastors are incompetent to counsel troubled people. Does it mean that bizarre behavior (along with garden-variety hostilities between parents and teens!) lies outside the scope of biblical wisdom?

Let me interact with this statement sentence by sentence.

"Psychologists do far more than engage in the practice of psychotherapy." Indeed they do, and some of these roles are uncontroversial, as discussed earlier. I, for one, am glad that a psychologist friend of mine does mental status exams on Air Force pilots before they are allowed fly. The thought of a drunken, suicidal, homicidal, delusional, or fatigued pilot flying an F-15 is not a happy one. And I'm glad that a psychologist friend of mine does mental status exams for residents in a nursing home. It helps to know if a person is disoriented and confused. But that said, psychotherapy is the money-making staple for most Christian psychologists.

Such counseling practice is legitimated by a great deal of popular writing and speaking. In fact, psychology's biggest influence in the Christian church at this time is *not* through psychotherapy but through classes, conferences, videotapes, radio shows, and best-selling books. The statement stresses the "service roles" psychologists have assumed within our culture. But it does not mention their biggest (and most questionable) role: teaching us about human nature, interpreting our problems, and teaching us their solutions. *Is* the driving force in human motivation the empty, needy self, a receptacle of needs that were not met by significant others? *Does* psychotherapy offer value-neutral objectivity and uniquely wise insight into what makes us tick, and uniquely wise strategies for living? These doctrines ("theories," "models") do not stand the test of Scripture. Typically, Christian psychologists simply teach secular models overlaid with some mention of God, Jesus, and the Bible. It is a curious, precarious development for the church when psychologists claim that they offer the deep answers to three critical questions: (1) Who *is right* in their interpretation of human beings and their problems? (2) Who *has the right* to work with people experiencing problems? and (3) Who *can make it right* and solve people's problems?

Psychologists' teaching role in offices, classrooms, and books ought to be highly controversial. But this letter glides over that question. Each of the examples cited also proves more dubious upon closer inspection.

"To whom would you take a six-year-old boy to determine whether he was emotionally and physically ready to enter first grade?" An educational psychologist might offer an accurate assessment and good advice. But you might also take your boy to his pediatrician to answer the physical readiness questions. Take him to the principal of the school and to kindergarten and first grade teachers for the other questions. They have dealt with hundreds of kids over the years. Other parents are also a terrific resource. Experienced people of many sorts can give you good advice to weigh into your determination of your child's readiness. And you, the parent, are going to make the final decision in any case. Even in assessment, no unique prerogative and authority attaches to the job title "psychologist."

"To whom would you turn if your wife became schizophrenic and ran screaming down the street? Would your pastor be able to deal with that situation?" This example is a scare tactic. Of course, most people are overwhelmed when facing bizarre behavior. But I know many experienced pastors and pastoral counselors who would deal effectively with such a situation. A level head and an action plan are not unique to psychologists. In fact, this is a curious example to use for several reasons. First, even in secular settings psychologists are usually not part of the crisis response team that first intervenes. If your wife's behavior and thinking became bizarre, help from a medical doctor, your family, the police, and your pastor (or other pastoral counselor) should enable you to do what can be done humanly. Second, psychotherapists' success with so-called schizophrenics is not noteworthy. Invariably, many factors play out in why someone breaks. The communal resources of a church can actually better provide for long-term counseling needs because one-on-one formal counseling is only a small part of a larger whole. All this said, in the midst of the crisis and its immediate aftermath, the love of level-headed family members and a safe "time-out" location often provide the most significant help of all.

"What if you wished to make a career change . . . and wanted an objective evaluation of your strengths and interests? Whom could you ask to help you?" A career counselor could provide interest and aptitude testing and knowledge of the job market. That person might be a psychologist but usually isn't. A pastoral counselor should be able help you think through your motives for considering a change as well as help you with other aspects of the decision-making process. People who know you well and people in your current and contemplated careers can also offer practical advice.

"To whom would you go to seek help with an adolescent who was extremely rebellious and resentful of his father?" This is bread-and-butter biblical counseling. Engage both the adolescent and the parents in counseling. Find out why and how the child is resentful and rebellious and whether or how the father is provoking him. Help them both to make necessary changes, patiently learning how to love and respect each other.

"In each of these instances, and in a hundred others, you should look for a psychologist whose first love and highest commitment is to Jesus Christ and to the Word of God. And how silly to say, 'There is no such thing.'" I honestly can't think of any instances, except perhaps intelligence testing from a school psychologist, where the title psychologist would be intrinsically significant. Biblically wise, case-experienced people from many walks of life might prove helpful in each of these instances. Such a person might happen to have the title of psychologist or psychiatrist, but he or she might just as easily wear the title of pastor, mom, teacher, physician, neighbor, or police officer.

In these cases and a hundred others, look for biblical wisdom, not a title. Though hard-won through experience in applying truth to life, such wisdom is available to all who seek it.

16   WHY I CHOSE SEMINARY FOR COUNSELING TRAINING

Should you go to a seminary or Bible college to train in counseling? Thirty years ago, this might have seemed like a nonsense question. Would you go to Virginia to study the geology of Vermont? Order a Big Mac at Burger King? Of course not. People went to seminary to study Bible, church history, theology, and preaching to become preachers, missionaries, chaplains, and Bible professors. But counseling? Serious one-on-one talking with people was the property of secular graduate schools. Seminary was about proclamation, not conversation.

But in the late 1970s, I *did* go to seminary to train in counseling. And – with appropriate cautions – I recommend the same today.[1] Though no counseling degree was offered at the time, the theology and Bible courses were strikingly relevant to a young man with counseling aspirations. I was taught about human nature; about suffering and God's providence; about the work of Christ's grace to forgive and remake us; about the way fallen thought suppresses true knowledge of self, God, and circumstances; and much more. Though most of the courses didn't make counseling applications in any detail, they were unmistakably about the "stuff" counseling deals with. What I learned of theology and the Bible, even of church history, has been as significant as my formal counseling courses for my maturing as a counselor.

CONVERSION TO CHRIST WITHIN A MENTAL HEALTH WORLD

Earlier in my life I had planned to go to secular graduate school in clinical psychology. I studied psychology in college, worked four years in psychiatric hospitals, and spent almost two years in psychotherapy myself. I embraced the claim that psychology offered the truth about people and that psychotherapy possessed the love and power to solve the ills of the human soul. But in the process of becoming a Christian, I became disillusioned with the secular psychologies and psychotherapies. Three things changed my mind and, eventually, changed the direction of my education and counseling practice.

First, I became increasingly conscious that the conflicts existing between psychological theories were fundamental, not incidental. The ground-breakers and system-builders were incompatible with each other, both personally and systematically. I studied Sigmund Freud, B. F. Skinner, Alfred Adler, Carl Rogers, and psychopharmacology. Those are five different "religions," and they treat each other that way! I was particularly intrigued by object relations psychology, existentialist psychology, Carl Jung, Anna Freud, Erik Erikson, Irving Yalom, Fritz Perls, and Abraham Maslow. From such masters, I initially created my own loose syncretism.

Over time, however, that syncretism proved unstable. The contradictory character of the component parts asserted itself. Who was right? Every theory seemed "sort of right" until the next theory put a different spin on the same observations or highlighted new ones to show that the previous theory was "quite wrong." The second generation theorists, therapists, and students-in-training like me often tended to be more tolerant, eclectic, and syncretistic. We tried to integrate incompatible views of human nature into a fuller, truer synthesis – or at least a workable personal approach. But principled eclecticism, like passionate commitment to one particular theory, still installs each person as his or her own ultimate authority, the founder of an idiosyncratic Grand Unified Theory. "Every man did what was right in his own eyes" is the way I would put it now. I increasingly questioned whether the psychologies really offered much beyond kindness and common-sense observations of people. Meanwhile, Christianity was increasingly making better-sense observations of people and speaking of a far deeper kindness.

Second, my experience in the mental health system fed a growing disillusionment and skepticism. I was working as a Mental Health Worker (MHW) on a locked ward at McLean Hospital outside Boston. One day a young woman named Mary slashed herself with a broken bottle. As we dressed her wounds and sought to calm her, she wailed inconsolably, "Who will love me? Who will love me? Who *could* love me? Who *could* love me?" Drugs eventually quieted her down. But her anguish and guilt made the psychologies I believed seem like thin gruel. Her distraught cry was realistic and heart-rending. Nothing I knew could really answer her, not her psychiatrist, medication, parents, job, boyfriend, or peers in the small group I led. We could manage Mary – sort of – but neither our theories nor techniques could really touch what ailed her. I now see that her cry of desolation could only find answer in the mercy and hope of Jesus, one thing that our theories, therapies, and institution made a point never to offer her.

Other experiences also contributed to my disaffection. It was remarkable that the staff member most effective with patients was a career MHW. He was the only staff member who had never gone to college or nursing school and the only MHW without aspirations to grad school. With love and firmness, he built real relationships and held people responsible for what they thought, said, and did. He did not treat them as helpless victims of trauma or mental illness. His method – common grace humanity – flew in the face of psychiatric theory, the institutional ethos, and my career plans.[2] But patients respected him, laughed with him, loved him and got mad at him. When they were in crisis, they wanted to talk with him.

After two or three years, it dawned on me that even our "successes" were at best mild. Some people "coped" a bit better after our help. But was it because psychological theory and therapy were true, good, and effective? Or was it because medication and a time-out from life took the edge off? And why was the readmission rate so high? And even if what we believed and did made some difference, was this simply because any organized theory about life works better than chaos and obvious delusion? Was it simply because human kindness works better than life in the jungle? At times I saw symptoms moderated, but I saw nothing that I could call deep, life-renewing change. The word "cope" pressed me down. It is a dismal word: life is hopeless ("vanity of vanities" Eccl. 1:2), but some people learn to cope better.

Third, I had no answer to my own need. Once "troubled" people are seen as people, not patients, they are not that different from the people who treat them. The differences are differences of degree, not kind. Staff members, too, had our relational breakdowns, our confusions, our escapes. We, too, lived out the "madness in our hearts" (Eccl. 9:3). We, too, saw our therapists and felt our quiet desperations – though we coped better. The more I observed, the thinner my theories seemed. The more I knew of myself and others, the more I saw that the human condition was better described in places other than the modern psychologies. I saw things in myself and our "patients" that I had read in Sophocles, Shakespeare, Dostoevsky, Kierkegaard, Kafka, Faulkner, Dylan Thomas, and T. S. Eliot. I found the human condition: sin and self-deception, love and candor, suffering and meaninglessness, joys and satisfactions, desire and disappointment, hubris and self-centeredness, humility and self-sacrifice, anguish and confusion, hopes and vain hopes, the looming of death, the longing for redemption. In time, to the praise of God, I found the human condition best captured – not only captured, but entered and redeemed – in Jesus Christ of the Bible.

I had long despised the Word of God and repressed the God of that Word. I came to Jesus Christ because the God of Scripture was merciful. He understood my motives, circumstances, thinking, behavior, emotions, and relationships better than all the psychologies put together. They saw only the surface of things, for all their pretension to "depth." He cut to the heart. They described and treated symptoms (in great detail, with scholarship and genuine concern), but they could never really get to causes. He exposed causes. They misconstrued what they saw most clearly and cared about most deeply. He got it right. They could never really love adequately, and they could never really reorient the inner gyroscope. God is love, with power. They – we – finally misled people, blind guides leading blind travelers in hopeful circles, whistling in the dark valley of the shadow of death, unable to escape the self-centeredness of our own hearts and society, unable to find the fresh air and bright sun of a Christ-centered universe. Scripture took my life apart and put it back together new. The Spirit of sonship began the lifelong reorientation course called "making disciples." The God of all comfort gave truth, love, and power. Christ exposed the pretensions of the systems and methods in which I had placed my trust. Even better, Jesus gave me himself to trust and follow.

WISE THEOLOGY, WISE COUNSELING

Although I went to seminary when the only counseling courses were a few basic electives, I learned much about Scripture, theology, history, and missions that profoundly shapes my counseling today. Biblically wise counsel is permeated with things not necessarily learned in "counseling" courses, but with basic facts of human existence:

- God sovereignly controls all circumstances. Every human being is continually dependent on and colliding with the one true God.
- The Lord evaluates and speaks to every aspect of human life.
- Our Father, Savior, and indwelling Lord is gracious, patient, and powerful. He works personally in individuals and groups.
- Sin inhabits and perverts every aspect of human functioning.
- Sufferings, difficulties, deceptions, and temptations in all their forms exist within God's purposes. He works to bring good out of things meant for evil and experienced as painful.

- Redemptive change is as far-reaching as sin and misery. Christ works change over the long haul, lifelong and progressive.
- The change that most matters and lasts longest is that into the image of Jesus. Such godliness is seen in the details of daily life – how we think, feel, talk, and make decisions.
- The Spirit and the Word are the prime change agents. God uses everything else, too, especially the body of Christ and our sufferings.
- All systems of psychological thought are affected by sin and must be critiqued by Scripture's view of the human condition and its cure. God's gaze and intentions are fundamentally different from those of fallen man.
- The imperatives to love and reach all people from "every nation, tribe, tongue, and people" (the stuff of evangelism and missions) also apply to one-anothering all individuals (the stuff of counseling ministry).
- Ministry, whether public or personalized, is a pastoral activity that incarnates and applies God's truth in love to real people.

Those truths are not truisms – though they can be misused and debased. They are the fabric out of which wise counseling is constructed. Oliver Wendell Holmes once said, "I would not give a fig for the simplicity this side of complexity, but I would give my life for the simplicity on the other side of complexity." The Word of Christ is that simplicity on the far side of every complexity. It can face and contain anything. Addison Leitch varied Holmes's words this way: "On the near side of complexity is simplistic. On the far side of complexity is simple." Biblical wisdom is the simple that probes and comprehends the complex, not the simplistic that ignores the complex.

Sure, Bible-sounding concepts can be made as simplistic and reductionistic as the worst pop psychology. And non-biblical concepts can quickly turn into labyrinths of complexity. The post-modern "multi-modal" pragmatism of most contemporary psychotherapists is finally an assertion of despair as to whether we can truly know anything. Christ, on the other hand, is simple, yet he speaks into every nuance. He imparts to us a simple gaze and clear thinking, letting us ponder every variation and ambiguity without losing our bearings. He teaches us how to be properly agnostic and self-critical, and yet to be valiant for truth. He forms in us an unwavering redemptive agenda and an indestructible hope, letting us enter any life, no matter how confused, sordid, anguished, violent, addicted, or terrified. He teaches us how to feel properly weak and overwhelmed, and yet to walk confidently. In a good seminary (and in a fine local church), I learned to give my life for such simplicity.

During my time at seminary, I learned to think about life biblically. I learned to know the innate dynamics of our disorientation and the invading dynamics of our reorientation. I learned the gifts and calling God had given me. I met people who loved God and counseled wisely, though they did not see themselves as "counselors." I learned the most important things about counseling as I observed and experienced God and godly people at work.

I then actually learned how to counsel by doing it: trial-and-error, asking for advice, talking over cases with others – with some basic orientation and ideas from counseling courses. If there had been a fuller counseling program in seminary, my learning curve could have been shortened. Systematic course work, observation, and ongoing supervision are valuable and desirable. But the heart of counseling was still available to me in a seminary that didn't yet have these things. A person can have all the education and the finest supervision in the world and never understand what counseling is really about. We can be expertly discipled into the wrong worldview. We can very skillfully and unwittingly mislead the people we counsel.

So what is the most important ingredient in counseling? Biblical wisdom. Truth and love becoming increasingly casewise. No seminary can guarantee the acquisition of such wisdom – far from it. And no secular counseling program – which, by definition, discards the "fear of the Lord" up front – can teach real wisdom. But a good theological education can provide the raw materials of counseling apart from counseling courses.

Combine that with personal honesty, the fellowship of wise people in a good church, taking opportunities to minister to others, and finding wise counselors for yourself, and your counseling wisdom grows. Good counseling courses, then, like good preaching courses, ought to help turn raw materials into more finished goods, connecting God's truth to real people.

Counseling Is a Theological Matter

A theological seminary to train in counseling? Today, this no longer seems absurd. Counseling programs and courses abound in seminaries. But should you go to a seminary to train in counseling? Let me offer a specific way to think about the question. I will propose a defining statement and then pose a series of questions.

Statement: You should consider attending a seminary to study counseling not simply because seminaries happen to offer counseling programs, but because *counseling is a theological matter*. Your integrity as a Christian who counsels hangs on grasping this core principle. Counseling programs in a given seminary may not live up to this principle. You have to keep your head no matter where you train.

Now the questions. First, *what is counseling?* From God's point of view, counseling is as broad as whatever proceeds from "the tongue." Our every word communicates values, intentions, and worldview; "the mouth speaks out of that which fills the heart" (Matt. 12:34). Counseling, then, is either wise or foolish. Some words are destructive, misleading, un-nourishing (Eph. 4:29a); others are constructive, timely, true, loving, grace-giving (Eph. 4:15, 29b). None are neutral.

More narrowly, counseling is any conversation *intended* to help someone solve a problem. A lawyer, a guidance counselor, a friend, a pastor, and a psychotherapist may each offer *counsel* (the explicit or implicit content) and do *counseling* (the relational and change processes). If you are thinking of studying counseling, you are likely most interested in the kinds of things that those last three counselors – the "peer," the "religious professional," and the "mental health professional" – do and say.

Second, *what purposes do those last three pursue, and what problems do they attempt to address?* Such people profess to care, to be objective and unbiased. Their stated purpose is to help you, not to get your money, exploit your sexuality, win your admiration, or prove themselves powerful, successful, or superior. Whether they prove wise or foolish, they will inevitably listen to hopes and fears, life's hardship and sweetness, loss and blessing, guilt and relief, confusion and clarity. They hear of good and evil, both what you do and what happens to you. They inevitably interact with the whole person: what you think and feel, what you've done and hope to do, and why. Such counselors – the sort most would-be "counselors" wish to become – deal with your *story.* In fact, they become players in the story. By word and deed, even by their line of questioning, they inevitably offer some form of editing or reinterpretation of your story. They deal with who you are, how you live, and what you face, not with the legal phrasing of your will or which college might admit you. They profess to help you by changing something about you as a person.

Now let's get even more specific. *What sense should counselors make of the problems they address?* That is the third foundational question. What's really happening in lives? What ought to change? What ought to be encouraged? All counseling is value-laden. Counseling is inescapably a moral and theological matter. To pretend otherwise is to be naïve, deceived, or deceitful. Whether implicit or explicit, theologies and counseling systems differ. All counseling uncovers and edits stories; what is the true "meta-narrative" playing out in human lives? Stories differ. All counseling must deal with questions of true and false, good and evil, right and wrong, glory and shame, justification and guilt. The answers differ. All counseling explicitly or implicitly deals with questions of redemption, faith, identity, and meaning. The redemptions offered differ.

Ponder this quotation from Martin Luther on the kind of redemption Jesus offers:

> This life therefore is not righteousness, but growth in righteousness; not health, but healing; not being but

becoming; not rest but exercise. We are not yet what
we shall be, but we are growing toward it. The process
is not yet finished, but it is going on. This is not the
end, but it is the road. All does not yet gleam in glory,
but all is being purified.

Luther here defined one possible goal for counseling. It is the
goal of *biblical* counseling. It is not the goal of any other form
of counseling. Of course, every form of counseling has some
analogous sense of process, of some problem to be resolved. But
the destinations, roads, and agents are different. Biblical ministry aims for the only personal growth process that finally matters and forever endures. It aims to restore the image of Jesus,
destroying sin and unbelief through the power of the Holy
Spirit, who puts love for God and man into human hearts. It
sustains sufferers by giving a specific kind of hope, hope
attached to a Person who daily bears us up. The Bible says that
he who began this work in you will bring it to completion on
the day of Christ Jesus, when every evil will be replaced by love,
joy, peace, and the rest (Phil. 1:6).

Secular psychological models employ some of the same
words Luther used: growth, healing, process. They would be
implausible if they were not somehow analogous to truth. The
lie always operates *sub specie boni*, under the aspect of good; the
plausibility of any counterfeit depends on its likeness to the real
thing. But the non-biblical cure of souls is animated by different goals and tells a different story. The same words mean quite
different things. Only one Counselor's gaze and intentions aim
for the destination Luther describes; only one Counselor walks
his children along the road Luther walks. May the great
Counselor make the under-counselors faithful!

We have circled back to the crucial statement that should
guide your decision about seminary: *Counseling is a theological
matter* – always. All counselors deal with the problems to which
the Bible speaks. By implication, they are either faithful or false.
I am speaking in principle, of course. Because of sin, counselors
and systems are more or less faithful, more or less false. Often
common grace brightens up secular models and practitioners

(though sometimes they are utterly false and wicked). Inevitably, remnant sin dims biblical models and practitioners (though by God's grace his children sometimes shine brightly). Only Jesus is utterly faithful, rich, and simple. You should aim to become a counselor who is more faithful and less false, full of riches and less impoverished, simpler and less simplistic or complicated. Seek the same from your training. Aim to learn counsel that expresses Christ's gaze and intentions rather than any other framework for making sense of life.[3]

ASK GOOD QUESTIONS

Should you go to seminary or Bible college to be trained in counseling? I believe that a good theological education is the education of choice. Naturally, I'm partial to Westminster Theological Seminary and CCEF, where I teach, here in Philadelphia. We have an experienced and unified faculty, and we offer degree programs in counseling. We are not alone. Interest in and commitment to biblical counseling is growing in the counseling faculties of a number of Bible colleges, Southern Baptist seminaries, and Reformed seminaries – and probably in other places of which I'm unaware. Do your research. You'll find that individual faculty members in many places want the Word of Christ to call the shots in personal ministry rather than simply augment secular psychological models with a bit of Christianese. Be humble and candid as you explore whether such intentions are fulfilled.

Ask good questions of schools. Ask students, graduates, and professors when you talk with them. As you reflect on a class you attended, as you read an article or book that the school points to as definitive, ask yourself, "What am I hearing?" Many kinds of questions can prove helpful. Here is a sampler:

- What counseling model do you teach? What authors and books are most influential and representative?[4]
- Run a case study by students and professors to test how counseling theory and methodology appear in action: e.g., What are the causes and cures of "low self-esteem," an "eating disorder," or bondage to pornography?[5]

- How is biblical truth actually used in the classroom? The counseling room? The representative article or book?[6]
- What is the relationship between counseling and evangelism? Between counseling and discipleship? Between counseling and preaching?[7]
- What ministries or careers do graduates find themselves prepared for?[8]
- What do you think about Meier New Life Clinics? Jay Adams? Larry Crabb? The *Journal of Biblical Counseling*? Psychoactive medications? A couple of representative secular psychologists? Demon-deliverance ministries?[9]
- What can be learned from secular psychology? From psychological research, personality theories, or psychotherapies? What are the dangers and cautions? Ask for examples and specifics.[10]
- What are the weaknesses of this program, and what is being done to correct them?[11]
- What counseling tradition is this school coming from historically, and in what direction is it heading?[12]

Just as you'll ask questions about other theological positions taught in a seminary or Bible college, so you ought to ask these sorts of questions about the view of counseling.

Many schools import alien ideas and methods into their programs or have an impoverished view of Scripture. They may have never thought through counseling ministry from the ground up according to Christ's intentions. The fact that so many seminaries now have "counseling" programs is a mixed blessing. Is the counseling consistent with sound biblical theology and pastoral methods? Are statements about Christ and counseling mostly window dressing, or do they reflect fundamental and growing realities?

You should know one more thing about seminaries and colleges, something that never appears in the catalog. Surprisingly often, the counseling and/or psychology department operates at cross-purposes to the theology, biblical studies, and preaching departments in the same school. They may contradict one another's views about human nature, suffering, God, and change. Ask professors and students in other departments how they view the counseling courses. Weigh the answers and consider the sources.

Choosing a school is a challenge. You must know what you are looking for to know if you have found it. These questions can help. Remember where this chapter began. The most valuable things you learn about counseling may come in your Bible and theology courses – as long as *you* do the hard work of application and never sector off the Word of God from human life. I'm grateful that I learned to counsel in a seminary that took the Word of God seriously in its counseling courses. I didn't have to unlearn many things later or continually sift what I was being taught. But though problems in a counseling department may be significant, they need not be fatal to a good and helpful education. Know what you're looking for.

God cares about counseling ideas and activities because counseling is a theological matter. He wants you to learn to do it wisely, and he blesses good counseling. You will find profound joys and worthwhile sorrows in face-to-face ministry. Talking with people one-on-one is as much the province of the church as preaching on Sunday morning. Consider theological education as the education of choice for counseling training. But make your decision with your convictions firm, your eyes open, and good questions on your lips.

17   AFFIRMATIONS AND DENIALS

Some 1500 years ago, the warrior-chief of a primitive Germanic tribe bluntly questioned a visiting missionary. "Why should I believe in this Jesus that you tell me about?" The man of God answered, "Because in Jesus Christ you will find wonder upon wonder – and all true."

That same Counselor is full of fresh wonders today. How do any of us come to serve him well? We must know some things.

We must *know* the wisdom of what God says. He speaks profoundly and comprehensively to the conditions of every person's life. He speaks with intent and power to change us:

> The law of the LORD is perfect, restoring the soul; the testimony of the LORD is sure, making wise the simple; the precepts of the LORD are right, rejoicing the heart; the commandment of the LORD is pure, enlightening the eyes; the fear of the LORD is clean, enduring forever; the judgments of the LORD are true; they are righteous altogether. . . . Let the words of my mouth and the meditation of my heart be acceptable in your sight, O LORD, my rock and my Redeemer. (Ps. 19:7- 9, 14)

Truth awakens us to reality.

We must *know* the gravity of our condition as human beings. We tend to defect. We are false lovers. We are traitors – compulsively, blindly. We want the wrong things. We are doomed. We need rescue from ourselves, from what we bring

on ourselves, from what others do to us. The twin evils of perversity and pain aren't a general theoretical problem. It's my
specific problem, and yours, and the other person's, too:

> This is an evil in all that is done under the sun, that
> there is one fate for all men. Furthermore, the hearts
> of the sons of men are full of evil and insanity is in
> their hearts throughout their lives. Afterwards they go
> to the dead. (Eccl. 9:3)

Sin and suffering are what's wrong.

We must *know* the sheer goodness of what our Father has
given us in Jesus Christ. To know Jesus in truth and love is to
find the one thing worth finding, the one lasting happiness,
the purpose of life:

> He will dwell among them, and they shall be his peo-
> ple, and God himself will be among them, and he will
> wipe away every tear from their eyes; and there will
> no longer be any death; there will no longer be any
> mourning, or crying, or pain; the first things have
> passed away. And he who sits on the throne said,
> "Behold, I am making all things new." (Rev. 21:3-5)

His mercies make wrongs right.

We must *know* our calling as children of such a Father. Jesus
announces his kingdom with the words, "Repent." That simply
means, "Change." His grace and truth get about the business of
changing us. We are called to live a new creation onto the stage
of history, into the details of our lives. We are called to change
and to change the world. We are called to build a wise community. We run a lifelong race of repentance and renewal, not just
individually, but all together. Jesus intends to teach us how to
live as "disciples" (changers, learners, students), so that we
become his instruments of change in the lives of others. The
Counselor full of wonders makes *Christianoi*, "Christ-people,"
apprentice counselors also full of wonders:

> Speaking the truth in love, we are to grow up in all aspects into him who is the head, even Christ. (Eph. 4:15)

We grow up, each and all.

We must *know* that God's way is qualitatively different from every other option available: other counsels, other schemas, interpretations, practices, and systems. The only sanity is to know Him-who-is. Anything else perpetuates our insanity:

> See to it that no one takes you captive through philosophy and empty deception, according to the tradition of men, according to the elementary principles of the world, rather than according to Christ. (Col. 2:8)

Truth operates differently from every other wisdom on earth.

We must know these things, live them, and minister this Christ to others.

Defining Counseling Faith and Practice

Attempts to define Christian faith and practice always arise in a context of controversy. These affirmations and denials are no exception. They are about "counseling." But a mental health system that knows no Christ dominates the counseling landscape and shapes the mind and practices of the culture. Even the "Christian" counseling field has largely taken its cues from the secular psychologies, as if Scripture did not really have much to say beyond religiosity and morality. But as we look more closely at life, it becomes clearer and clearer that Scripture is *about* counseling: diagnostic categories, causal explanations of behavior and emotion, interpretation of external sufferings and influences, definitions of workable solutions, character of the counselor, goals for the counseling process, configuring the professional counseling structures, critique of competing models. These are all matters to which God speaks directly, specifically, and frequently. He calls us to listen attentively, to think hard and well, and to develop our practical theology of conversational

ministry. These affirmations and denials attempt to state what
our Lord sees, says, and does, making pointed application to
contemporary questions about counseling.

Section I treats the sufficiency of Scripture. Unless God lies,
he has given us the goods for developing systematic biblical
counseling, just as we have the goods to develop preaching,
teaching, worship, mercy, and missions. What do we need to
counsel others well? We need a comprehensive and penetrating
analysis of the human condition: Section II. We must bring to
bear effective solutions, equally penetrating and comprehensive, the Redeemer who engages persons and problems appro-
priately: Sections III and IV. We must embody counseling in
social structures: Section V. We must have a standpoint from
which to interact with other systems of counseling: Sections VI
and VII. Scripture teaches us how to know and do these things
so that we might care for souls the way Christ does.

I. TRUE KNOWLEDGE ABOUT PEOPLE AND COUNSELING PRACTICE

We affirm that the Bible is God's self-revelation in relation to his
creatures, and, as such, truly explains people and situations.

We deny that any other source of knowledge is authoritative
for explaining people and situations.

We affirm that the Bible, as the revelation of Jesus Christ's
redemptive activity, intends to specifically guide and inform
counseling ministry.

We deny that any other source of knowledge is authoritative
to equip us for the task of counseling people.

We affirm that wise counseling requires ongoing practical
theological labor in order to understand Scripture, people,
and situations. We must continually develop our personal
character, case-wise understanding of persons, pastoral skills,
and institutional structures.

We deny that the Bible intends to serve as an encyclopedia
of proof texts containing all facts about people and the
diversity of problems in living.

We affirm that the ideas, goals, and practices of counseling must cohere explicitly with the historic creeds, confessions, hymns, and other wise writings that express the faith and practice of the church of Jesus Christ.

We deny that the wisdom of the past sufficiently defines the issues of counseling ministry for today, as if the requisite wisdom were simply a matter of recovering past achievements.

II. The Givens of the Human Condition and the Scope of Biblical Truth

We affirm that human beings are created fundamentally dependent on and responsible to God. People can only be understood when these realities control the counselor's gaze.

We deny that any form of autonomy severs people from dependency on God.

We deny that any form of determinism neuters moral accountability to God.

We affirm that the ideal for human functioning is faith working through love. Such love for God and neighbor is the standard against which to specifically understand what is wrong with people. It is the goal to which counseling must specifically aspire.

We deny that any other standard or goal is true.

We affirm that evil, done by us and happening to us, is the fundamental and pervasive problem in living. Our own sin, in all its facets and dimensions, is primary and self-generating. The circumstances that happen to us provide both provocative context ("trials and temptations") and just consequences ("reap what you sow") for our moral response but do not determine the quality of our moral response.

We deny that any other diagnostic system is valid, universal, or penetrating.

We deny that nature and/or nurture determine the quality of our moral response.

We affirm that the Scripture defines and speaks to the gamut of problems in living for all people in all situations.

> *We deny* that biblical truth is limited to a narrow sphere of "religious" or "spiritual" beliefs, activities, persons, emotions, and institutions, separated from the other spheres of daily life.
>
> *We deny* that any particular realm of human life can be sectored off as the unique province of the theories, practices, and professions of the modern psychologies.

III. The Solution to the Sin and Misery of the Human Condition

We affirm that the Bible teaches, invites, warns, commands, sings, and tells the solution for what troubles humankind. In the good news of Jesus Christ, God acts personally. In word and deed, he redeems us from sin and misery through the various operations of his past, present, and future grace. God uses many means of grace, including the face-to-face conversations of wise counseling.

> *We deny* that any other solution or therapy actually cures souls and can change us from unholy to holy, from sinners to righteous, from insanity to sanity, from blindness to sightedness, from self-absorption to faith-working-through-love.

We affirm that God's providential common grace brings many goods to people, both as individual kindnesses and as social blessings: e.g., medical treatment, economic help, political justice, protection for the weak, educational opportunity. Wise counseling will participate in and encourage mercy ministries as part of the call to love.

> *We deny* that such goods can cure the soul's evils. When they claim to cure the human condition, they are false and misleading, competing with Christ.
>
> *We deny* that Christless counseling – whether psychotherapeutic, philosophical, quasi-religious, or overtly religious – is either true or good. Their messages are essentially false and misleading, competing with Christ.

IV. THE NATURE AND MEANS OF CHANGE

We affirm that the growth process for which counseling must aim is conversion followed by lifelong progressive sanctification within every circumstance of life. Our motives, thought processes, actions, words, emotions, attitudes, values – heart, soul, mind, and might – increasingly resemble Jesus Christ in love for God and other people.

> *We deny* that there is any method for instantaneous or complete perfection into the image of Jesus Christ. The change process continues until we see him face to face.

> *We deny* that the processes and goals labeled self-actualization, self-fulfillment, healing of memories, meeting of psychological needs, social adaptation, building self-esteem, recovery, and individuation describe valid aims of counseling, though they may evidence analogies to elements of biblical wisdom.

We affirm that the Bible explicitly teaches the fundamentals of counseling method by precept and example. Through speaking the truth in love, we act as tangible instruments of God's grace in the lives of others.

> *We deny* that the modern psychotherapies rightly understand or practice wise counseling methodology though they may evidence analogies to elements of biblical wisdom.

V. THE SOCIAL CONTEXT AND SCOPE OF COUNSELING MINISTRY

We affirm that the Spirit and the Word create the church of Jesus Christ and that the people of God should provide the personal, social, and institutional loci for speaking truth in love.

> *We deny* that the mental health professions and their institutions have the right to claim any sector of problems in living as their particular prerogative. Even those who suffer mentally-disabling medical problems need godly counseling as part of comprehensive care.

We affirm that the aims, content, and means of counseling ministry are of a piece with public ministry, the spiritual disciplines, and mercy ministry. These are different aspects of the one redemptive ministry of Christ.

> *We deny* that the persons and problems addressed by the activity termed "psychotherapy" fall outside the intended scope of the ministry of Christ in word and deed.

We affirm that the primary and fullest expression of counseling ministry occurs in local church communities where pastors effectively shepherd souls while equipping and overseeing diverse forms of every-member ministry.

> *We deny* that the institutional forms and professional roles of the mental health system provide a normative and desirable framework for counseling ministry.
>
> *We deny* that current forms of church life and conceptions of the pastoral role are necessarily adequate and normative as vehicles to train, deliver, and oversee effective counseling ministry. The body of Christ needs institutional reformation, development, and innovation.
>
> *We deny* that parachurch and other cooperative forms of counseling ministry in the body of Christ are inherently wrong.

VI. GOD'S PROVIDENCE AND THE INTERPLAY BETWEEN HIS COMMON GRACE AND THE INTELLECTUAL-PRACTICAL EFFECTS OF SIN

We affirm that numerous disciplines and professions can contribute to an increase in our knowledge of people and how to help them. Scripture teaches a standpoint and gaze by which believers can learn many things from those who do not believe.

> *We deny* that any of these disciplines and professions can align and constitute a system of faith and practice for wise counseling.

We affirm that a commitment to secularity distorts disciplines and professions fundamentally and pervasively. People who do not think and practice in submission to the mind of Christ will misconstrue the things they see most clearly and will miscarry in matters about which they care most deeply and skillfully.

We *deny* that secular disciplines and professions are entirely benighted by the intellectual, moral, and aesthetic effects of sin. The operations of God's common grace can cause unbelievers to be relatively observant, caring, stimulating, and informative.

We *affirm* that the personality theories are essentially false theologies, and the psychotherapies are essentially false forms of the cure of souls. Even more descriptive and empirical psychologies are significantly skewed by secular presuppositions. Their findings need reinterpretion by the biblical worldview.

We *deny* that psychological research, personality theories, and psychotherapies should be viewed as "objective science" as that term is usually understood. Nor should they be seen as extensions of medicine and medical practice.

VII. GOOD NEWS FOR PSYCHOLOGIZED PEOPLE IN A PSYCHOLOGIZED SOCIETY

We *affirm* that mature, presuppositionally consistent, loving, and efficacious biblical counseling will be a powerful evangelistic and apologetic force in the modern world.

We *deny* that the most important part of the church's interaction with the modern psychologies is to discover what can be learned from them.

DISCUSSION OF AFFIRMATIONS & DENIALS

On the face of it, Scripture is *about* counseling. It's about God's diagnosis and cure of the human condition. It's about trustworthy love and being known by another. It's about a growing self-knowledge, making sense of life's circumstances and our reactions. It's about an interpersonal process (a "walk" with God and one another) and specific personal and relational changes. It's about how you understand or misunderstand life, how you behave or misbehave. It's about what you believe, desire, fear, trust, and value. It's about how you act, talk, and feel. It's about your relationships to others and to Him-who-is. Scripture is also about untrustworthy, inaccurate, misleading, and false messages and persons, about other counsel and other counselors. Seen this way, the dynamic and the subject matter of Scripture is recognizably the activity we term "counseling" – but with a dramatic twist.

What most people think of as "counseling" is controlled by the enculturated habits of the modern mental health system. A designated professional comes with credentials: an advanced degree and state licensure. This professional claims to offer expertise in supposedly objective, non-religious ideas and techniques, the substance of modern psychologies or psychiatries. A designated and diagnosed patient/client suffers from a syndrome with a medical-sounding label and seeks help. The two parties enter into a formal, consultative relationship. Together they explore the world of the patient: experiences, thoughts, feelings, behaviors, motives, relationships. In some fashion, the professional mediates interpretations and solutions that claim the authority of science and/or medicine. This fee-for-service exchange occurs in a time-out from real-life social relationships. There is a fundamental asymmetry between doctor and patient, expert and client, healthy and sick.

Against this backdrop, the Bible seems to say little if anything about "counseling." The concordance doesn't seem to mention the parties involved, the diagnostic labels, the interpretations of causality, the proposed solutions, the methods, and the institutional structures necessary for effective counseling. It's true that the mental health system does not appear. But cut through the cultural assumptions, and you see something very different. The Bible is *about* what counseling is about, from beginning to end.

FOUR BIBLICAL DISTINCTIVES

The Bible is odd music, however. God plays in a different key, with different instruments, even on a different scale. Here are four examples among many that could be cited.

First, God subverts the asymmetries of the doctor-patient relationship (Luke 5:31). He views us all as basically more alike than different. All of us are "sick" with the madness in our hearts. Each of us needs the "physician." The insane, the criminal, the perverted, and the addicted share a common human nature with the sane, the law-abiding, the upright, and the self-controlled. And each of us – even the weakest, poorest, and most troubled – is capable of helping any of us in some way when grace gifts and masters us.

Second, the Bible is too straightforward about relationships to be esoteric or mechanical in its "counseling techniques." It's about how we all counsel each other for good or ill in our daily interactions. Do you love wisely? Do you enter in? Give? Care? Do you really know people? What are you looking for? What do you ask? What do you say? How do you say it? When? What the Bible says about "the tongue" changes both formal consultations and chit-chat. Speaking truth in love is neither a mysterious art nor a set of techniques. And "counseling" is always measured against the scale of speaking truth in love.

Third, when Jesus himself uses medical language – we are the sick, he is the doctor – it's a vivid metaphor, not biomedical reality. The "sick" have "diseases" of unbelief, pride, and sins. The "doctor" "heals" by loving well: speaking, dying, rising, and giving. We turn and listen and learn to love. The Bible paints all life as inescapably religious and relational. The kinds of problems psychotherapy deals with are particularly obvious examples: unpleasant emotions, destructive behaviors, broken relationships, distorted thinking, life's multitude of sufferings and disappointments. Nature and/or nurture do not finally explain any of these things; healing the body or the society will not finally cure any of them. In all these ways, we are "sick" at heart and beset by a "sick" world, compromised by evils within and without. Jesus enters into such problems. It's difficult to imagine a Jesus impressed by therapeutic claims to objective, a-religious knowledge (which requires erasing the living God from human affairs). It's difficult to imagine a Paul yielding to a professional's claim to specialized authority and prerogative over the problems of living: "I'll help people with the religious dimension, but I'll defer to you for all the real life problems."

Fourth, God's vision of counseling is not limited to the individual: *your* problems, the one-on-one conversation. It's not even limited to a family system: *our* marriage conflicts, the one-on-two-or-more interaction. God deftly locates individual and family within a wider social-communal context. Scripture has an unerring instinct for speaking to the interplay between the one, the few, the many, and the all. The most public and "impersonal" counsel (a sermon or book reaching thousands) has fundamental continuity with the most private and personal counsel. His purposes are finally communal: a people who love. Individual renewal is both product and producer of communal renewal. It's easier to witness this interplay in action (read Ephesians!) than it is to nail down. A person is neither a discrete psychological entity nor an undifferentiated nonentity within a sociological collectivity.

Those four differences alone would revolutionize the counseling field. People who see this come to understand themselves, other people, and life circumstances *coram Deo*. And they see God in Christ.

A COUNTER-CULTURAL PROCESS

The Bible's vision of "counseling" is stunningly different from current cultural habits and received wisdom. It's a bigger and better way of thinking about "counseling." And it's true. The culture says, "This is how it's done. We've always done it this way" (though historical memory tends to be very short). But Scripture drastically changes the paradigm – to put it mildly. Counseling doesn't just inhabit clinical settings, nor is it the property of upstart professions practicing in wealthier countries. God's view of counseling cuts more deeply, applies more widely, aims differently, lasts longer, matters more. You live or die based on the counsel you listen to – and the counsel you give. Counseling is not just for those who "need counseling." It's not just something that "professional counselors" do with "counselees." You can't escape being involved in the Bible's view of the counseling process. It's happening all the time whether you know it or not. You are doing it to others; others are doing it to you – today, every day, informally, and (very occasionally) formally. All people influence others by what they believe and want; all are influenced by the thoughts and intentions of others. All of human life is by definition counseling. "The tongue" is a counseling instrument. Every human interaction, from the most trivial to the most formal, arises from the nexus of meanings, values, and intentions that controls the hearts of the participants.

Counseling is never about neutral, objective knowledge. We human beings always "impose values" on each other, covertly if not overtly. No one can avoid this. The questions you ask (or don't ask), the emotions you feel (or don't feel), the thoughts you think (or don't think), the responses you give (or don't give) tip your hand and overflow from your heart. Therapists aren't just skillful or clumsy, caring or callous. Their counseling is never neutral and objective. They are committed, and those commitments come out continually. Their counseling is always either true or false. They lead others into knowing Jesus or into some other image of the human being. Diagnostic categories, interpretative schemas, analyses of causality, ideals of health, particular advice, and personal character are not neutral.

God alone is objective, and he is fiercely committed to his point of view. He evaluates every word out of every mouth because these register the thoughts and intentions of every heart as for or against him. Counseling is not a matter of neutral technical expertise and an inherently legitimate professional role. In principle, counseling is either wise or perverse, just as all human beings are either sages or fools, trust-worthy or untrustworthy, whatever their professional roles. In principle, counseling either leads truly or leads astray. Graduate education and professional role are not the decisive criteria. The deciding factor is wisdom, and the organizing center of wisdom is the fear of Christ. God plays by a different set of rules – and he makes the rules. Theories of human nature and formal counseling practices are a subset of much bigger things. They are subject both to the terms in which those bigger things tran-spire and to evaluation by him with whom we have to do.

The designated counselors in a culture (or church) may do a poor job of communicating what life's all about. They may tell misleading stories, mislabel life, and instill myths to rule the hearts of those they counsel. But God's story is still what's playing in real time. His story is not about coping better. You either die to yourself and live for Another, or you live for yourself and die. It's not about meeting your needs but about turning what you think you need upside down. It's not about locating causality in historical circumstance or biological process but about your heart vis-à-vis God in Christ. Moment by moment, we worship, love, desire, fear, serve, believe, and trust either God or something that is not God. God's story is not about finding refuge and resources in yourself, in other people, or in psychopharmacology. It's about finding Christ in real times and places, the only Savior able to deliver you from what's really wrong with you and your world.

By words and actions, God counsels all people. He reveals us for what we are and either changes our ways or hardens us in our ways. Paul's letter to the church in Ephesus offers an exemplar and synopsis of the contents, methods, and institutional context for "curing souls." As Christ's personal agent, Paul communicates what's on the mind of the Searcher of hearts. He dissects the human condition. As a recipient of grace, he extols the one comprehensive solution, the living Lord we are made to know, love, and serve, and from whom we learn to know, love, and serve others.

For spiritual vitality, the church of Jesus Christ must submit to God's definition of both counsel (the content) and counseling (the activity). It is our deepest delight and sanity to rightly understand counselor and counseled, problems and solutions, process and goal. The wise church submits to the God whose wraths and mercies are pure and takes our definitions of trouble and comfort from him.

In the providence of God, the twentieth century brought an extended crisis and conflict about counseling. In the West, a persuasive redefinition of the ideas, practices, and institutions of "pastoral care" has taken place. The cure of souls has become secularized by the intentions of modern personality theories, by the practice of mental health professions, by the biases within medical and psychological research. Can we actually comprehend human life with no reference point outside ourselves? Can we actually redeem human life with no savior outside ourselves? The attempt to do just that essentially dehumanizes patients, clients, and subjects. It purges life of its true context (God in Christ). It redefines the true drama (Are you good or evil? Do you serve truth or lies?). It misconstrues causality (Your heart is active towards God amid the trials and opportunities God's providence arranges in nature and nurture). It ignores the true outcome (Will it be life or death forever?). It represses the one essential truth (To know you, the only true God, and Jesus Christ whom you have sent).

THE CHURCH'S RESPONSE

How has the church responded to this massive cultural effort to redefine the ideas, practices, and institutions that cure our souls? The church has largely been the borrower and subordinate, not a thoughtful and decided alternative. Where the church has not borrowed, it has tended to react, offering religious pat answers and quick fixes for nothing less than the human condition: pragmatic moralism, demon deliverance, ecstatic pietism, doctrinal navel-gazing, semi-magical views of prayer and of Bible quotation. Is there a thoughtful and decided alternative both to secularity and to religiosity?

With all my heart, I believe that such an alternative is in front of us. It's for the taking. And it's for lifetimes of work and working it out. What must we do to capture the centrality of Jesus Christ for helping people to grow up into the only true sanity? How will we all learn to live in the radical extrospections of faith and love, rather than be lulled by the inward-curving inertia of sin? How will we deal gently with other sinners, offering our own mercy and grace to help in time of need? How will we find meaning, safety, and sustenance in our own sufferings? How will we offer others aid and refuge in theirs? How will we reconfigure "helping" relationships to serve as instruments of the only enduring wisdom? How will capturing a true counseling vision also reconfigure worship, preaching, teaching, writing, evangelism, mercy ministry, one-anothering, parenting, friendship?

The mind of Christ looks at life differently than our culture does. His words and deeds aim in a different direction. The scope of Scripture's purposes and sufficiency includes those relationships that our culture labels "counseling" or "psychotherapy." These affirmations and denials have attempted to state and to guard the lineaments of such convictions. This is a rough draft proposal for a creed: "We believe. I believe. Here I stand."

THE PURPOSE OF A CREEDAL STATEMENT

What is the purpose of such a creedal statement? The affirmations and denials assert convictions. They define a position, make distinctions, and draw boundaries, always amid the swirl of some controversy. That last phrase is important. No statement of faith ever arises in a vacuum. For example, when some people start teaching, "Jesus isn't really God," *then* the church is forced to get about the business of defining and defending the Trinity and the nature of the God-man, Jesus Christ. You must understand the background questions and debates that this statement of faith aims to address. It invites people to commit to principles that unite us in practicing, developing, and defending a way of thought and practice worthy of the name "biblical counseling."

What controversies operate in this case? Two huge questions clamor, one in the foreground, the other in the background. Front and center is a positive question: "What *does* Christian faith and practice have to say about counseling relationships and the resolution of human problems?" The backdrop is a question about our historical and cultural location: "How *does* Christian faith and practice relate to the research, theories, therapies, and institutions of modern secular psychologies?" In a nutshell, what is the Faith's psychology, and how does it relate to the psychological faiths?

The church has been wrestling with these questions for over 100 years. One sort of answer has been adopted by the "integrationist" movement within evangelical Protestantism since the 1950s. Though there are many debates within integrationism, the common result has been to "baptize" secular concepts, methods, and professional structures. Here's a common example. A fee-for-service, state-licensed psychotherapist adopts a need theory of human motivation and puts major emphasis on exploring how needs for love and self-esteem weren't met within the family of origin. Personal problems (anger, anxiety, addictions) arise from a historical determinism. The counselor defines the goal of counseling as changing self-talk and meeting psychological needs. Is the insertion of some form of religious teaching – some mention of God and Jesus – enough to make such counseling "Christian"? I think not. The core Christian worldview (e.g., the active, responsible heart vis-à-vis God) has been erased or distorted by the theoretical, methodological, and institutional commitments of the practitioner. Some overt content may gesture in a Christian direction ("Jesus meets your needs"). But the false structures of secular thought still exert decisive control.

Negatively, these affirmations and denials stand against false interpretations of the human soul – the secularistic reductionism of the personality theories. They oppose misleading attempts to cure the sin and suffering of the human condition – the man-centeredness of the psychotherapies. And they oppose false understandings of the very phenomena/data of human experience – the nature/nurture determinism that skews the social, behavioral, and medical sciences. They oppose the integrationist approaches that attempt to wed secular psychologies and Christian faith as if this were both the way Christianity relates to culture and the way Christ would have us approach counseling.

Positively, these affirmations and denials establish the importance of a biblical starting point. God's gaze rightly interprets phenomena (things secular research and personality theories distort by their biases). God's intentions rightly realign human problems (things secular psychotherapies misunderstand and misdirect). We believe that we understand people accurately only to the degree that our thinking aligns with God's way of seeing and interpreting life. We believe that we truly help people only to the degree that our counseling aligns with God's redemptive intentions and activity.

SIX LIMITATIONS

A statement of faith serves some good purposes but not all purposes. What are the limitations of a creed such as this? Here are six limitations.

First, it is a work of a fallible person (and people) seeking to make good sense of the Bible. Any proposed statement of faith needs ongoing scrutiny and correction. We must try a statement on for size. Test it by Scripture. Test it in the midst of life and ministry. Test it against the questions and challenges that get raised. During the process, we find out what proves true, what's missing and needs to be added, what's murky and needs clarification, what's mistaken and needs to be altered.

Second, it takes a step away from the actual text of Scripture. Creeds are necessarily abstract. They lack the personality, color, fire, and drama of the Word living and written. There are no names of people and places, no events, no weather, no marriages or bereavements, no victories or defeats, no "he said, she said," no fears or joys. A good creed defines the fence line that encircles the garden of life. We live and minister within the garden, enjoying the fruits. But a good fence in the right place protects us from straying into the loco-weed and keeps predators out.

Third, it takes a step away from actual life and ministry. Within the pages of this book, I *love* the opening chapter on Psalm 119. It blazes with life, joy, and need. I don't *love* this more bony, abstract chapter. But I need it. We need it if we are to keep in mind where we ought to be heading. A creed lacks the immediacy and personality of the Word lived and the Word communicated by word and deed in counseling. But within the fence line, ministry thrives in the garden of honesty made over by truth and love.

Fourth, it is abbreviated. Every assumption, intention, and implication isn't necessarily spelled out. It has a limited goal. No creed connects its assertions with all other aspects of

Christian truth and life. It may not capture the balance of living wisdom because the discussion gets marked by current events, controversies, and vexed questions. So, a creed is the end point of one sort of labor and the starting point for many others. The purpose of the rest of this book is to do a little of that further work.

Fifth, it is open to misinterpretation. Friends of a statement may draw false conclusions and implications. They may get preoccupied with the fence line and lose sight of the garden of life within. Foes of a statement may wrench its intended meaning, caricature and mock it. They may read it through a lens of suspicion and so misread it. As with any piece of writing, it takes hard work to understand what is at stake, what is intended, what is actually being affirmed, what is being opposed, and what it all means.

Sixth, it is no guarantee of the wisdom, godliness, character, or consistency of adherents. Right commitments are hugely significant. They ought to set us in the right direction and correct us when we drift. But church history demonstrates that no profession of faith and practice ensures perfect wisdom in faith and practice! We can all be ignorant, narrow-minded, clumsy, or compromising. Sometimes we live up to what we profess; sometimes we do better than what we say we believe; sometimes we do worse. Adherence to openly stated beliefs means something but not everything.

Conviction alone simply waves a flag. Eventually it degrades into sloganeering and hardens into triumphal defensiveness. But as the intellectual ramifications and practical implications are lived out, we'll have something. As the Faith's psychology is demonstrated to be penetrating, comprehensive, adaptable, and efficacious, we'll have something. Such counseling wisdom will edify the teachable – and even persuade the skeptical. The church needs persuading. And the church needs training to live and counsel the content. The surrounding culture also needs persuading. The matters confessed in these pages will shine in their glory when adorned with humble, tender, bold, and efficacious ministry that actually cures souls.

The goals of this chapter are necessarily modest (except for the hope of conquering the world!). These affirmations and denials cannot begin to communicate the countless positive details of what it means to counsel in the grace and truth of Jesus Christ. But they can at least serve as a beginning, an articulation of what must be worked thoroughly into our faith and practice. These words are up for criticism, debate, and refinement as well as being up to embrace. This is a *proposal*, a current best effort. I sincerely believe it can be improved with nothing good lost and much good gained.

COMPANIONS ON THE LONG MARCH

Those like myself whose imagination far exceeds their obedience are subject to a just penalty; we easily imagine conditions far higher than any we have really reached. If we describe what we have imagined we may make others, and make ourselves, believe that we have really been there.
– C. S. Lewis, *The Four Loves*

This has been a down-to-earth book, getting at practicalities of daily life. What are you listening for? What questions do you ask? What do you say? How do you say it? How do you allocate your time? What do you pray for? What is church life all about? At the same time, this book has actually been a work of the imagination. It imagines what should be and suggests where to pour our energies for the future. It imagines a day when "Christian" and "church" correlate to the simplest and most profound wisdom. It imagines human interactions that are sensible, powerful, probing, true, loving, and good in every way. Calling this book a "work of the imagination" doesn't mean I think it is a delusional fantasy or a utopian fiction! What I mean is that these things have not been fully realized in our own lives, in our local churches, or even throughout church history. We have a long walk ahead to bring our obedience up to our imagination.

There are times when I read Ephesians 3:14 to 5:2 and think, "We have no idea what this will look like when it comes

to fruition – and yet it will seem utterly familiar. It will be everything we've always wanted. We are *so* far away from this, yet we
have already tasted it, and want more. Unless God lies, all
church history, all the work of the Spirit, every word of
Scripture, every wise sermon, and every wise conversation have
been pushing in this direction."

There are times when I read this spectacular "Ephesians 4+"
and wonder if we are even Christians, if our church is even a
church, if church history has any links to the New Testament,
if God is really doing something good beyond all comprehen-
sion! The gap is so enormous. But then I realize that Ephesians
4+ is not just a vision that makes our achievements look very
small; it also offers explicit directions for the long journey to
bridge the gap. This vision of mutually constructive relationships is both promised and commanded by God. These are the
things that the Maker of heaven and earth has promised to
work in us and to work out through us. This means the transformation of the inner and outer workings of individuals and
communities. This is our highest joy and God's highest glory. If
the tasks of faithful imagination have been done well, what
we've talked about should seem so close you can almost touch
it, so real that you've had a sweet taste of that already. So right
and realizable that you can't imagine giving yourself to any
competing vision of "counseling" or "church."

FIVE STAGES OF DEVELOPMENT

I see five stages of development in the maturing of such wisdom in the cure of souls. These are stages that individuals go
through as we grow up to make our particular contributions.
These are also stages that churches, denominations, and eth-
nic/linguistic groups go through. Each reader of this book (and
his or her social setting) is somewhere within these five stages.

All of us come with history and experience, with ways of
understanding life's problems, and church, and counseling. *Stage
one is seeing a new vision for what can and ought to be.* Believe it or
not, the church should be outstanding in counseling. The cure
for what most deeply ails us exists . . . should exist . . . could exist.

Biblical truth is the deepest interpreter of the human psyche: we are laid bare before the eyes of the One who searches hearts and gets final say. Christ's mercy is exactly what people need, not in theory, not for religiosity, but in the bitter and delightful realities of life. Only the power and promise of God can deal with the evils that operate within us and that come upon us. In your experience, have churches, theologies, sermons, counselors, and ordinary Christian people failed to reach deeply enough into your personhood, pains, and perversities? Have they been flustered, rigid, or ineffectual? Have they skimmed over, mishandled, or even savaged the difficulties of your life? Has the Christianity package offered pat answers (i.e., functional falsehoods, however true in principle, when you need illuminating truth and love)? Have you been offered quick fixes (i.e., well-intended formulas when you need to learn how to live honestly lifelong)?

When you see the vision for biblical counseling wisdom, you realize that it doesn't have to be this way. The Christian faith continually reforms, revives, and redeems the defects in our understanding and practice of Christian faith. The Lord himself continually reforms, revives, and redeems us for his name's sake. (He just happens to take longer than we wish!)

How will you react to this vision? Are you indifferent? Afraid? Threatened? Hostile? Skeptical? Cynical? Or are you delighted and curious? *Stage two is commitment to that vision:* "I agree that this is what God and Scripture intend. Jesus Christ ought to cut deeper than any other approach to counseling. He made us and knows us. He saves us. He'll judge every thought, word, motive, and action. I may not know what it will look like and our church may not do it very well yet, but it's the right way to go." Vision and commitment can happen in a matter of minutes (though it may take years). I caught this vision and embraced it as delightfully true in 1975, during the first couple of months after coming to faith. After years in the psychotherapeutic world, I found that Christ turned my life upside down. Then I started to see that he turned the whole world upside down: *everything* was God-centered, not man-centered. That meant that counseling needed a fundamental realignment to inhabit the real world, not the world fabricated by unbelief.

After agreeing, what do you do? Some people seem to stop at commitment to the vision. Perhaps it seems too difficult to learn how to be redemptive, to speak truth in love in ways that actually help people. It's easier to get polemical and triumphalistic: "I'm right; everybody else is wrong." *Stage three is to get training.* Read books and articles. Sit under teaching. Pursue a course of study. Learn from people who know more than you. Learn how they treat people and approach problems. Talk with people who disagree with you or who don't know what they think. Listen hard to their perceptions, questions, and experiences. Struggle through your own troubles in the light of Christ. Your anger, joys, anxiety, and discouragement, your successes, escapism, and sufferings, are all God's context for making theory real. Biblical wisdom grows to handle whatever comes at it. Training always takes a lifetime because we are disciples of the Master who is making us over. My own training continued on through seminary, reading hundreds of books, enjoying scores of friendships, and seeking to honestly live what I believe. One pleasure in looking back over thirty years is to see what I have learned in just the past year, the past five years, the past decade.

So you've read books, attended conferences, perhaps gotten a master's degree, talked with lots of people. Now what? Your knowledge is not tested, not deepened by experience, not made effective. *Stage four is to develop skill.* You need experience with people, "the human documents," as Anton Boisen put it so well. There are no shortcuts in developing counseling skills that actually help people. To be wise, you must know people. Talk with them. Get a feel for them. Try to help others (and as you fail and succeed, keep learning why one or the other occurs). Talking to a depressed person for the very first time is a far different conversation from the one you'll have when you've cared for ten depressed people and seen some dark lives blossom. After ten years of working with people in conflict, you'll be wiser than in the first year. If you're growing in skill, you'll learn to love people better: you'll be more patient, more caring, more personal, more generous. You'll have a deeper and a wider knowledge of how people work, so you'll get to the crux of things more deftly. You'll know better how God's truth works in people's lives, so you'll speak more wisely into their experience: you will be more thoughtful, piercing, true, creative, personal, and encouraging. You'll know better how to help others make the hard, practical choices for faith and love that will rearrange their lives. All this only comes by doing over many years.

You've learned some things about helping people in their struggles. You've got some know-how – and, if you're honest, a deepening awareness of your fundamental powerlessness. You're more able to help others and more aware that you're unable to help anyone, but for the grace of God. *Stage five takes an increasing leadership role.* God gives us different gifts, experiences, limitations, and callings. I see three forms of leadership that typically emerge in experienced people. These are three necessities if biblical counseling is to become indigenous in any particular nation, people group, denomination, local church, or other ministry. Somebody must take the lead. Good leaders take the *next* step necessary for wise ministry to flourish.

THREE FORMS OF LEADERSHIP

First, skillful counseling ministry (stage four) is itself a form of loving leadership. But God usually intends such skills and knowledge to be passed on to others. One form of leadership is to train, supervise, advise, and consult with others who want to learn to counsel well. For many years, whenever I faced a perplexing counseling situation, I would stop in and chat with a wise older pastor. He had a knack for sizing up what I was facing. He would give me two or three practical things to think about or do: a fresh perspective, a line of questioning, a relevant Scripture, some ways to deepen the relationship, a story, a possible action plan, affirmation that I was on the right track. He was helpful every single time. If you've learned some things about helping people with their troubles, you've got something to give to other aspiring helpers.

Second, God gives leadership gifts for developing institutions, structures, and programs. The conversations of ministry need contexts for ministry. Leaders get people and activities organized. Counseling wisdom demands many forms of institutional development. For example, local churches will create many ways of structuring counselor training, oversight, and ministry practice. Particular life problems will call for different social structures: different staffing, training, setting, funding, time frame, biblical emphases, and so forth. Good leaders create structures appropriate to the need. For example, the needs of the lonely and elderly are different from the needs of teen-aged girls with eating disorders, or of middle-aged couples amid marital conflict, or of ex-cons and ex-addicts. The chapter, "Counseling Is the Church," sketched out some of the ways leadership can flourish in creating and maintaining institutions.

Third, we always need intellectual leadership. Biblical wisdom is a practical theological labor that will not be complete until the end of history. God will raise up leaders to teach, write, develop ideas. Teaching is always needed to bring those being trained up to speed with current wisdom. The person who will stand on your shoulders needs a boost so that each generation does not have to reinvent the wheel. And fresh intellectual work is always needed to deepen our insight and broaden our range of efficacy.

For example, our current models for understanding people, problems, and Scripture may be faulty or underdeveloped. Our skills may be imbalanced. The problems that counselors must address continually mutate like new strains of flu. Each new variation challenges us to apply biblical truth in a fresh way. Furthermore, our culture's theories about counseling continually mutate, raising new challenges to the adequacy and accuracy of our grasp on biblical truth. Each new idea sounds plausible, even persuasive, in its context. We must continually evaluate those voices, theories, practices, and institutions. They bid for the ears of people so that they might shape hearts and lives according to *their* vision of reality. God's vision must always be reunderstood, reapplied, and restated. Biblical counseling is an ongoing practical theological task in which leaders are needed.

How will all this look in your life? In your local church? In your denomination or group of churches? In your country?

God gives vision: Ephesians 4+ is realized on the stage of life. God works commitment: the Shepherd has a compelling voice. God calls us to learn: other people can teach us in person or in print. God gives jobs to do, people to love: we grow in love as we seek to help. And God raises up leaders who work to build up people, institutions, and ideas.

Perhaps you are thinking about all these things for the first time. Perhaps you are in a position of leadership already. Perhaps you are somewhere in the middle. In any case, my hope and prayer is that our God will fulfill all your desires for goodness and the work of your faith with power.

NOTES

PREFACE: GOOD INTENTIONS

1. David Powlison, *Seeing with New Eyes: Counseling and the Human Condition through the Lens of Scripture* (Phillipsburg, NJ: P&R Publishing, 2003).

PART I: SPEAKING TRUTH IN LOVE

1. The closest thing to a companion textbook is *Instruments in the Redeemer's Hands: People in Need of Change Helping People in Need of Change* by Paul David Tripp (Phillipsburg, NJ: P&R Publishing, 2002). Readers familiar with that book will discern within my pages various outworkings of Tripp's Love-Know-Speak-Do. I trust that our fundamental similarity of outlook will make our books reinforce each other, giving confidence that Scripture presents a coherent, highly adaptable model for counseling ministry. I trust that our differences of personality and application will stimulate readers to value and to develop the varied individual expressions of God's one wisdom. The recognizably *same* image of Christ comes out somewhat *different* in each one of God's children. One of the beauties of the biblical model is that unity and diversity both flourish!

CHAPTER 1: SUFFERING AND PSALM 119

1. Add to these the nouns for my identity ("servant") and your name ("LORD").
2. Verse 115, a brief aside, is the only break from this pattern.
3. Consider such passages as Psalms 10:6, 11; 14:1-4; 36:1-4; 53:1-4; Eccl. 9:3; Jer. 17:9; Rom. 3:10-18. Consider the first great commandment with its total claim on everything going on inside us. Consider the descriptions of what God sees when he looks at us: 1 Chron. 28:9; Heb. 4:12-13; Jer. 17:10. We are opaque to ourselves until God tells us what he sees.
4. Ex. 34:28, Deut. 4:13, 10:4 use the wider term *words*, not the narrower

commandments, when they refer to the ten components of the "words of the covenant."

5. In the next section, Strand 4, we will also hear shouts of joy.

CHAPTER 2: THE FACTS OF LIFE

1. Richard Sibbes (1577-1635) was a Puritan pastor. Quotation is from *The Soul's Conflict, and Victory Over Itself by Faith,* XV:vii:6, in *The Complete Works of Richard Sibbes,* Vol. 1, (Edinburgh: James Nichol, 1862), p. 200.

2. Robert C. Roberts, *Taking the Word to Heart: Self & Other in an Age of Therapies* (Grand Rapids: William B. Eerdmans, 1993) provides a provocative discussion. An excerpt and summary were published in *The Journal of Biblical Counseling* ("Psychology and the Life of the Spirit," 15:1, 1996, pp. 26-31).

3. John Calvin's piercing phrase in *Institutes of the Christian Religion,* III:iii:9, in John McNeil, ed., *Library of Christian Classics,* Vol. XX, (Philadelphia: Westminster Press, 1960), p. 602.

4. J. C. Ryle, *Holiness* (London: James Clark, 1952), p. 70.

5. From Bob Dylan's "When You Gonna Wake Up?" on *Slow Train Coming,* 1979.

6. From John Newton's hymn that begins "I Asked the Lord" (sometimes titled, "These Inward Trials").

CHAPTER 3: HEARING THE MUSIC OF THE GOSPEL

1. Frederick Faber, "Hark! Hark, my soul!" 1854.

CHAPTER 6: THINK GLOBALLY, ACT LOCALLY

1. From *The Best of C. H. Spurgeon* (Grand Rapids: Baker, 1979), p. 218; cited in Anthony Ruspanti, ed., *Quoting Spurgeon* (Grand Rapids: Baker, 1994), pp. 133-134.

2. Richard Baxter, *The Reformed Pastor* (Edinburgh: Banner of Truth, 1974), p. 61.

3. Joel Beeke, "William Perkins on Predestination, Preaching, and Conversion," in Peter Lillback, ed., *The Practical Calvinist* (Great Britain: Christian Focus Publications), p. 204.

4. Edward T. Welch, *When People Are Big and God Is Small: Overcoming Peer Pressure, Codependency, and the Fear of Man* (Phillipsburg, NJ: P&R Publishing, 1997).

CHAPTER 9: HOW DO YOU HELP A "PSYCHOLOGIZED" COUNSELEE?

1. The entire *Diagnostic and Statistical Manual, Fourth Edition* (DSM-IV)

does something similar. The more thoughtful practitioners —and DSM-IV's authors!—know full well that these are not "diagnoses" at all. They don't describe "things." A broken bone, pancreatic cancer, or viral pneumonia are things that people can "have." But people don't "have" oppositional disorder, borderline personality, adolescent adjustment disorder, or post-traumatic stress syndrome. They "do" such things. These categories simply describe a few typical patterns of behavior, emotion, attitude, thinking that are particularly unhappy and disruptive for everyone involved. They say nothing about causality. They are simply "syndromes," a group of things that often occur together.

CHAPTER 11: COUNSELING *IS* THE CHURCH

1. An earlier version of some of this article appeared in my "Questions at the Crossroads" (Mark McMinn and Timothy Phillips, eds., *Care of the Soul*, Downers Grove, IL: InterVarsity Press, 2001), pp. 23-61.

CHAPTER 15: DO YOU EVER REFER?

1. It's worth noting that many people committed to biblical counseling hold degrees in fields built upon secular counseling theories and methods. They happen to have education and experience in psychology, medicine, social work, or education – just as many people committed to secular counseling models happen to have degrees in divinity/theology!

2. This question is trickier than it first seems, especially when a psychiatrist has been trained to view all life problems as essentially organic. For example, when the experience of anxiety is explained as a genetically-linked generalized anxiety disorder; when homosexuality is affirmed as a genetic predisposition; when heavy drinking is credited to the disease of alcoholism; when eating disorders are labeled a genetically-based obsessive-compulsive disorder; when deep sorrow and distress are defined as clinical depression; when mood-, thought-, and behavior-altering drugs are the answer to all that ails us, then the organic component has obliterated more significant components. See T. M. Luhrmann's *Of Two Minds: The Growing Disorder in American Psychiatry* (New York: Knopf, 2000) for a discussion of tensions created by hyper-biologizing. See my "Biological Psychiatry" (in *Seeing with New Eyes*, Phillipsburg, NJ: P&R, 2003, pp. 239-251) for a discussion from a biblical counseling point of view.

3. This quotation was presented in a form letter sent out by a Christian ministry to answer those who question the validity of psychology.

CHAPTER 16: WHY I CHOSE SEMINARY FOR COUNSELING TRAINING

1. An earlier and abbreviated version of this article appeared in *The 1994 Seminary & Graduate School Handbook*, (Evanston, IL: Berry Publishing Services, 1994), pp. 22-24, 48.

2. Peter Kramer's *Moments of Engagement* contains fascinating portrayals of such a-theoretical, a-professional common grace humanity in the practice of a psychiatrist (New York: W. W. Norton, 1989; Kramer is also author of *Listening to Prozac*).

3. With a clear and comprehensive biblical worldview, one can fruitfully pursue further studies in almost any subject, including the social, behavioral, and medical sciences. For example, our counseling faculty here at CCEF and Westminster Seminary includes people whose advanced theological degrees have been supplemented by doctorates in neurophysiological psychology, medicine, sociology of culture, history and sociology of science and medicine, and developmental psychology.

4. This question helps you "locate" a department on the spectrum of views and practices. It reveals whether a department has a unified point of view or is eclectic but does not evaluate the information you discover or familiarize you with the lay of the land. If a department is unified, how do you evaluate that working psychology of counseling? If it is eclectic, is such diversity intentional or unwitting? Of course, reality is often untidy, but in principle, there are four options: unified around biblical wisdom; unified around a defective model; an intentional collection of diverse viewpoints; or a mere hodge-podge.

5. This question allows a person to reveal core functional commitments in an anecdotal way. Is the human heart passive and externally determined (e.g., unmet needs) or fundamentally active (e.g., first great commandment)? Is personal history determinative, or does it provide a context in which the active heart reveals itself? Are labels merely descriptive (and often problematic), or do they bear explanatory and objective freight? Is Christ's past, present, and future work immediately essential, or is it restricted to an ancillary spiritual dimension? Does Scripture define the story and the categories that life plays out, or is some other storyline calling the shots? Is Scripture viewed moralistically (and either denigrated or misused), or is it viewed as revealing a Person to know, trust, and obey?

6. *How much* is Scripture about what counseling is about? *In what way* is Scripture about what counseling is about? Both the "useful spiritual resource in combination with psychology" view and the "exhaustive source of proof texts for any problem" view are problematic. Scripture is far more comprehensive than the syncretistic first view. God's distinctive point of view is significantly at odds with research, personality theories, and therapies. His revealed purposes are far more than a "resource" to augment psychotherapies. And Scripture is far more adaptable and demanding than the biblicistic second view. God's prophets and apostles both model and mandate that we do the hard practical theological work necessary to bring abiding truth to bear in fresh situations. Is Scripture viewed properly as sufficient and constitutive for counseling ministry, or is it treated either as deficient or as magical?

7. These questions reveal basic and often implicit assumptions about human nature, Christ, counseling, the church – and about the activities labeled "evangelism," "discipleship," and "preaching." Do people with counseling problems inhabit an essentially and pervasively God-centered, Christ-dependent world? Or do they inhabit a world that transpires rather autonomously from God in Christ?

8. This is one of those "actions speak louder than words" questions that often show whether a program treats serious counseling as part of wise and robust ministry, or whether serious counseling is the prerogative of mental health professionals, with ministry as a somewhat debased junior partner.

9. I don't intend that there is one "right answer" or "right point of view" on these names and institutions or that you should get into a debate. Your purposes are information gathering, to enable a wise decision. Get your informants to talk about how *they* see the lay of the land in counseling, and you'll learn invaluable things that will help you decide with your eyes open. Where are they informed? Ignorant? Balanced? Bigoted? Penetrating? Superficial? The questions and criticisms they raise about others may give you helpful questions to ask those others. One way to get at those "representative secular psychologists" is to ask the person, "Who do you consider to be the most significant secular psychologists, and how do you assess them?" On my own, I'd probably ask about cognitive-behavioral psychology, Maslow's hierarchy of needs, Sigmund Freud, and family systems therapy because these have been so influential among evangelical Christians.

10. Every sort of "Christian" counselor – mainline Protestants teaching CPE, Rosemead psychotherapists, Jay Adams, Martin Bobgan (and everyone else) – believes that Christians can learn something from secular psychologists. How does this person define that "something," and what priority does he give it? The first question is general and can bring out how a person defines "Psychology" and its relationship to Christian faith. The second question teases apart the more scientific from the more theological and pastoral aspects of "Psychology" (though even research is far from neutral, usually being predicated on social or biological determinism). It alludes to the diversity of views and activities lumped under a heading as contentless as "Religion." It reveals how well a person has thought through subtleties and nuances. Even more important than theoretical generalities, what actually happens in practice and emphasis? The "dangers and cautions" question often reveals whether someone thinks of Christian faith as a "gaze," a unified and distinctive worldview that interprets and reinterprets everything, or whether one thinks of Christianity as a "screen" or "filter" that weeds out some particularly bad things (such as endorsements of sexual immorality or New Age spirituality), while leaving many ideas and practices unexamined and intact.

11. Candid humility and self-criticism are always assets and aids to an inquirer seeking to make a fair assessment; bravado and salesmanship are always unsavory.

12. Schools are usually in process, not static. Just as with progressive sanctification of the individual (or progressive degeneration!), direction counts for a lot. You can also tailor this question to an individual teacher to bring out his or her own sense of pilgrimage: "Where have you come from? Where are you? Where are you going? What matters to you?"

Scripture Index

Genesis
1 – 19
6:5 – 18

Exodus
3:11-12 – 43
4:11 – 145
20:2 – 137
34:6-7 – 19

Numbers
6:24-26 – 30

Deuteronomy
4:13, 10:4 – 195
31:6 – 70

1 Kings
17 – 122

2 Kings
4 – 122

1 Chronicles
28:9 – 195

2 Chronicles
16:12 – 122

Psalms – 50, 124
10:6 – 195

11 – 195
14:1-4 – 195
19:7- 9, 14 – 167
23 – 13, 30
31 – 51, 128
32:8-9 – 85
35:12-14 – 122
36:1-4 – 195
53:1-4 – 195
57:1-3, – 59
57:3, 4, 6 – 59
57:5 - 59
57:7-11 – 60
103 – 13
118:6 – 70
119 – 7, 11-31, 184
119:132 – 64
121 – 13, 65
127:2 – 29
131 – 30
139 – 13

Proverbs – 85
3 – 105
8 – 105
10:19 – 85
14:10 – 54
18:2 – 15
18:28 – 85

Ecclesiastes
1:2 – 156
9:3 – 22, 38, 156,
   168, 195

Isaiah – 78
38 - 122
40-66 – 77
40:11 – 78
40:12-13 – 78
43:4-6 – 77
44:18, 20 – 78
49:13-16 – 77
50:4-10 – 77
52:13-53:12 – 77
61:1-3, 10-11 – 77
66:23-24 – 77

Jeremiah
17:9 – 195
17:10 – 195

Ezekiel
36:26 – 6

Matthew
12:34 – 160

Mark – 105
6-9 – 106
7-11 – 105

7:6-7 – 106
10 – 106
10:1 – 108
10:4 – 106
11:17 – 106
19 – 106

Luke
5:31 – 177
6:21-49 – 60
8 – 75

John – 134, 137
15 - 75
15:1-2 - 51
21:25 – 137

Acts
6:1-5 – 73
13:14-41 – 94
14:14-17 – 94
17:16-34 – 94

Romans
3:10-18 – 195
5:3-5 – 121
5:5, 8:15 – 42
8:26 – 139
8:31-34a – 42
12 – 60
15:4 – 43

1 Corinthians
10:11 – 43
10:12-13 – 76
10:13 – 135
13 – 60

2 Corinthians
1:4 – 121, 135
5:14-15 – 42
5:15 – 87
12 – 122
12:9-10 – 121

**Ephesians – 30, 42,
50, 79, 81, 178**
1-6 – 81
1:15-23 – 124
3:14 - 5:2 – 3, 187
3:14-21 – 124
4 – 2, 3, 60, 80, 99,
115, 116, 130, 188,
193
4-6 – 134
4:15 – 53, 79, 160, 169
4:15-16, 25, 29 – 86
4:17 – 79
4:17 - 5:10 – 50
4:17-32 – 79
4:22 – 79
4:29 – 53, 79
4:29a – 160
4:29b – 160
5:14 - 100
6 – 80

Philippians – 12
1:6 – 162
1:9-11 – 124
2:12-13 – 51

Colossians
1:9-14 – 124
2:8 – 169
3:17 – 53

1 Thessalonians
5:14 – 76, 131

2 Thessalonians – 1
1:11 – 1

1 Timothy
4:16 – 142

Titus – 50
2:11-15 – 50, 52

**Hebrews – 68, 69,
70**
3 – 2
3:12-14 – 118, 130
4:12-13 – 195
4:15 – 106, 139
5:2 – 61
5:2-3 – 130
12:5-6 – 51
13 – 71
13:5 – 70
13:5b-6 - 69
13:5-6 – 70, 71
13:6 – 71

**James – 12, 120,
121**
1:2, 5 – 121
1:2 – 62, 137
1:3 – 121
1:13-16 – 146
1:18-22 – 86
3:16 – 62
5 – 122
5:13-20 – 120

1 Peter – 43, 60
1:6-8 – 121
4:1-3 – 121

1 John
3:2 – 43

Revelation
20:4 – 44
21:3-5 – 168

DAVID POWLISON, M.DIV., PH.D.

Dr. Powlison edits *The Journal of Biblical Counseling,* counsels and teaches in CCEF's School of Biblical Counseling, and teaches Practical Theology at Westminster Theological Seminary. He has written *Power Encounters: Reclaiming Spiritual Warfare; Competent to Counsel? The History of a Conservative Protestant Anti-Psychiatry Movement; Seeing with New Eyes: Counseling and the Human Condition Through the Lens of Scripture* and numerous articles on counseling. David and his wife, Nan, have a son and two daughters.